BBC

VOLUME 25

D1124826

PHILIPPIANS COLOSSIANS and FIRST and SECOND THESSALONIANS

Edward P. Blair

ABINGDON PRESS
Nashville

This book is printed on recycled, acid-free paper.

Library of Congress Cataloging-in-Publication Data

Cokesbury basic Bible commentary.
    Basic Bible commentary / by Linda B. Hinton . . . [et.al.].
        p.   cm.
    Originally published: Cokesbury basic Bible commentary. Nashville: Graded Press, © 1988.
    ISBN 0-687-02620-2 (pbk. : v. 1 : alk. paper)
    1. Bible—Commentaries. I. Hinton, Linda B. II. Title.
[BS491.2.C65   1994]
220.7—dc20   94-10965
                                                                                    CIP

ISBN 0-687-02645-8 (v. 25, Philippians–2 Thessalonians)
ISBN 0-687-02620-2 (v. 1, Genesis)
ISBN 0-687-02621-0 (v. 2, Exodus–Leviticus)
ISBN 0-687-02622-9 (v. 3, Numbers–Deuteronomy)
ISBN 0-687-02623-7 (v. 4, Joshua–Ruth)
ISBN 0-687-02624-5 (v. 5, 1–2 Samuel)
ISBN 0-687-02625-3 (v. 6, 1–2 Kings)
ISBN 0-687-02626-1 (v. 7, 1–2 Chronicles)
ISBN 0-687-02627-X (v. 8, Ezra–Esther)
ISBN 0-687-02628-8 (v. 9, Job)
ISBN 0-687-02629-6 (v. 10, Psalms)
ISBN 0-687-02630-X (v. 11, Proverbs–Song of Solomon)
ISBN 0-687-02631-8 (v. 12, Isaiah)
ISBN 0-687-02632-6 (v. 13, Jeremiah–Lamentations)
ISBN 0-687-02633-4 (v. 14, Ezekiel–Daniel)
ISBN 0-687-02634-2 (v. 15, Hosea–Jonah)
ISBN 0-687-02635-0 (v. 16, Micah–Malachi)
ISBN 0-687-02636-9 (v. 17, Matthew)
ISBN 0-687-02637-7 (v. 18, Mark)
ISBN 0-687-02638-5 (v. 19, Luke)
ISBN 0-687-02639-3 (v. 20, John)
ISBN 0-687-02640-7 (v. 21, Acts)
ISBN 0-687-02642-3 (v. 22, Romans)
ISBN 0-687-02643-1 (v. 23, 1–2 Corinthians)
ISBN 0-687-02644-X (v. 24, Galatians–Ephesians)
ISBN 0-687-02646-6 (v. 26, 1 Timothy–Philemon)
ISBN 0-687-02647-4 (v. 27, Hebrews)
ISBN 0-687-02648-2 (v. 28, James–Jude)
ISBN 0-687-02649-0 (v. 29, Revelation)
ISBN 0-687-02650-4 (complete set of 29 vols.)

94 95 96 97 98 99 00 01 02 03—10 9 8 7 6 5 4 3 2 1

MANUFACTURED IN THE UNITED STATES OF AMERICA

Contents

Outline

Philippians

I. Introduction (1:1-11)
  A. Greeting (1:1-2)
  B. Thanksgiving and prayer (1:3-11)
II. Body of the Letter (1:12–4:20)
  A. The advancement of the gospel (1:12-26)
    1. Paul's imprisonment (1:12-14)
    2. Paul's Christian opponents (1:15-18)
    3. The coming verdict (1:19-26)
  B. The church at Philippi (1:27–4:9)
    1. Imitating the spirit of Jesus (1:27–2:11)
      a. The threats to unity (1:27–2:4)
      b. Jesus Christ as source and pattern (2:5-11)
    2. The Philippians' mission (2:12-28)
    3. God's helpful servants (2:19-30)
    4. The true way of salvation (3:1-21)
    5. Models for appropriate behavior (4:1-9)
  C. The Philippians' gift (4:10-20)
  D. Concluding greetings and benediction (4:21-23)

Colossians

I. Introduction (1:1-14)
   A. Greetings (1:1-2)
   B. Thanksgiving (1:3-8)
   C. The prayer (1:9-14)
II. Body of the Letter (1:15–4:6)
   A. Christ versus the cosmic powers (1:15–2:23)
      1. The supremacy of Christ (1:15-23)
      2. Paul preaches Christ's supremacy (1:24–2:5)
      3. Transition (2:6-7)
      4. Victory over the elemental spirits (2:8-15)
      5. Regulations of the elemental spirits (2:16-23)
   B. Heavenly versus earthly life (3:1–4:6)
      1. The new life in Christ (3:1-4)
      2. Putting off the old nature (3:5-11)
      3. Putting on the new nature (3:12-17)
      4. Rules for the Christian household (3:18–4:1)
      5. Counsels on prayer and witnessing (4:2-6)
III. Conclusion (4:7-18)
   A. Greetings from Paul and associates (4:7-17)
   B. Authentication and benediction (4:18)

First Thessalonians

I. Introduction (1:1-3)
II. Body of the Letter (1:5–5:24)
   A. The Thessalonians' conversion experience (1:4-10)
   B. The ministry at Thessalonica (2:1-12)
   C. Imitators of the Judean churches (2:-16)
   D. After leaving Thessalonica (2:17–3:10)
   E. Prayer for the Thessalonians (3:11-13)
   F. Personal sexual morality (4:1-8)
   G. Love and work in the community (4:9-12)
   H. Destiny of the Christian dead (4:13-18)
   I. The coming of the Day of the Lord (5:1-11)
   J. Counsels for church life and worship (5:12-24)
III. The Conclusion (5:25-28)

Second Thessalonians

I. Introduction (1:1-4)
II. God's Righteous Judgment (1:5-10)
III. The Coming of Christ (2:1-14)
IV. Paul's View of Last Things (2:15–3:18)

Introduction to Philippians

The Church at Philippi

According to the book of Acts, Paul founded the church at Philippi on his second missionary journey, probably in A.D. 50. He crossed over the Aegean Sea—from Troas in the province of Asia (modern western Turkey) to Neapolis in Macedonia and on to the nearby Philippi—in response to a nighttime vision at Troas (Acts 16:9-10). Silas, Timothy, and possibly Luke (Acts 16:10) were with him.

Philippi, the most important city of the first district of Macedonia in Paul's time (Acts 16:12), had been built (or rebuilt) about the middle of the fourth century B.C. by Philip II of Macedon, the father of Alexander the Great. The city had become part of the Roman Empire after Rome's defeat of the Persians in 168 B.C. After 42 B.C. it was enlarged by Mark Antony and Octavian (Augustus), settled with Roman colonists, made a Roman colony governed by "Italian law," and blessed with all the privileges Rome bestowed on citizens who lived in its colonies.

The city, located in a fertile area fed by copious springs and with gold and silver mines nearby, lay astride the *Via Ignatia*, the main road connecting Rome with Byzantium in the East. The inhabitants were mostly Romans and Macedonian Greeks, with some Jews as well.

The religions of the city were many, centering in the

worship of Roman, Greek, and Thracian gods and goddesses, deities from Phrygia and Egypt, and Yahweh of the Jews.

Whether there was a Jewish synagogue at Philippi is uncertain. Acts refers to a *place of prayer* by the side of a river, where some women had gathered (16:13). Since Jewish synagogues were sometimes built close to water for convenience for ritual washings, a small synagogue may have stood there.

The first convert at Philippi was a Gentile woman, a God-fearer (*worshiper of God*, Acts 16:14) called Lydia. (For more information about God-fearers, see the Glossary of Terms.) Apparently Lydia was a seller at Philippi (and elsewhere) of purple-dyed cloth, made at Thyatira in Lydia (south-central Asia Minor). It may be that the name *Lydia* means simply *the Lydian*, and that she had an unknown personal name. (It is possible, but not probable, that this name was *Euodia* or *Syntyche*, and that she was one of the objects of Paul's entreaty in Philippians 4:2-3.) She offered her home to the missionaries as a place of residence and as the gathering place of the fledgling church (Acts 16:15, 40).

Women seem to have had a prominent part in the life and work of the Philippian church, even in the proclamation of the gospel (Philippians 4:3). This role accords with the general status of women in Macedonia, where they played an unusually important role in the political, religious, and social life of the province.

How long the missionaries stayed in Philippi is unknown (according to Acts 16:12), probably a few weeks. The membership, besides Lydia and her household, included the converted jailer and his family (Acts 16:27-34), Epaphroditus (Philippians 2:25), Euodia, Syntyche, and Clement (Philippians 4:2-3). The names indicate that the church was largely Gentile.

Paul's mission at Philippi was terminated as a result of an exorcism that affected the pocketbook of slave owners

PHILIPPIANS–2 THESSALONIANS

and led to a hearing before the magistrates and a subsequent beating and imprisonment (Acts 16:16-24). The charge was that the Jewish missionaries were troublemakers who were unlawfully turning Romans into proselytes (Acts 16:20-21). Paul might have revealed his Roman citizenship in order to escape beating and imprisonment without a proper trial before the proconsul of the province, but he did not do so. He may have wished to embarrass the local magistrates and thereby gain a more favorable position for the church (Acts 16:35-39). He later called his treatment at Philippi *shameful* (1 Thessalonians 2:2 NRSV; NIV = *insulted*).

Through the missionaries a vigorous church was raised up at Philippi, one that Paul trusted implicitly and one that made a unique contribution to his subsequent ministry (Philippians 1:5, 7; 4:14-16).

Place and Date of Writing

Acts records only three of Paul's prison experiences: at Philippi (16:23-40); at Caesarea (23:35; 24:23, 27); and at Rome (28:16, 20). But Paul speaks of more imprisonments than his opponents had experienced (2 Corinthians 11:23); and Clement, a Roman Christian, wrote (about A.D. 95) that Paul was in prison seven times. Many modern scholars have argued that to the three in Acts we should add one in Ephesus and perhaps one in Corinth.

The arguments are weak for an imprisonment in Corinth, but one at Ephesus is quite possible. First Corinthians 15:32, Acts 20:17-19, 2 Corinthians 1:8-10, and data in Philippians (and Philemon) offer support for such a conclusion.

If Paul was in prison in Ephesus (about A.D. 55), this city's relative closeness to Philippi helps us understand Paul's many exchanges with the Philippian church while he was confined. These exchanges are: News of Paul's arrest reached Philippi (Philippians 4:14); the Philippians sent a gift by Epaphroditus to aid him (2:25; 4:18); news of Epaphroditus's illness is carried back to Philippi (2:26); word comes to Paul and Epaphroditus concerning the Philippians' distress over Epaphroditus's illness (2:26); Paul hopes to send Timothy to Philippi and to receive a report back from him (2:19) and to go to Philippi himself (2:24).

If Paul had written the letter to the Philippians from Rome or Caesarea, so many exchanges with the Philippians while he was in prison seem difficult or unlikely. Journeys between Ephesus and Philippi could be made in about a week, whereas trips between Rome and Philippi (some 800 miles) and Caesarea, which is even farther from Philippi, would require a month or more.

Other arguments exist for Ephesus as the place of origin. There was a praetorium (the governor's residence) at Ephesus (Philippians 1:13), and those of *Caesar's* (NIV; NRSV = *the emperor*)household (4:22) could mean slaves and freedmen in the governor's service there. Also, the language, style, issues addressed, and concepts of Philippians bear some similarities to those in First and Second Corinthians, letters written at Ephesus or shortly thereafter.

Scholars who argue for Rome or Caesarea as the place of writing of Philippians point out that the Ephesian imprisonment is only hypothetical. The two-year period Paul was in prison both in Caesarea (Acts 24:27) and Rome (Acts 28:30) allows plenty of time for the exchanges with the Philippians noted above. Furthermore, the references in Philippians to the praetorium and Caesar's household connect more naturally with Rome or Caesarea (Acts 23:35). The best reason used by the advocates of Rome as the place of origin is the fact that in Philippians Paul seems to be awaiting a final life-or-death decision (1:20-26; 2:23). He would not have expected a final decision at Ephesus or

Caesarea, since, as a Roman citizen, he had the right of appeal to Caesar's court in Rome.

At present, equally good reasons can be cited in support of Ephesus, Rome, or Caesarea. Fortunately, the exact place of origin is not crucial to an understanding of the message of Philippians.

The Unity of the Letter

There is considerable roughness in the flow of thought in the letter. The sudden outburst in 3:2-3 is surprising. Also, 3:1 seems to connect logically with 4:4, making the intervening material appear intrusive. The farewell and benediction of 4:4-9 could well end the letter. But a long section about Epaphroditus and the Philippians' gift, which would appropriately appear near the beginning of the letter (or at least in connection with 2:19-30), is tacked on. And why doesn't 2:19-30, with its practical concerns, come at the end, according to Paul's usual practice?

Many scholars have concluded that two or three letters were combined into our present letter by someone later than Paul. Their reasons are, in part, the roughness noted above; the likelihood that Paul wrote more than one letter to his favorite church; the fact that Second Corinthians appears to have been compiled by a later editor from at least two letters addressed to the Corinthians; and a reference by the second-century Christian martyr Polycarp to "letters" written by Paul to the Philippians.

Various attempts, not always agreeing in details, have been made to identify these letters. The hypothesis of two letters usually assigns to the first letter 3:2–4:23 and to the second 1:1–3:1. The hypothesis of three letters goes: letter one—4:10-20; letter two—1:1–3:1; 4:2-9, 21-23; and letter three—3:2–4:1.

Many scholars argue for the unity of the letter. They point out that Paul was writing an informal letter, not a logical treatise. He may have been interrupted in his dictation and begun again without careful consideration of logical sequence. Such breaks in logical sequence appear in other letters he wrote (for example, Romans 16:17-20; 2 Corinthians 2:14-15). Furthermore, why would a later editor arrange the supposed letters in the illogical fashion we find here? And what happened to the original openings and conclusions of the previous letters?

Since scholars have not agreed on the question of the letter's unity, it is best to study the letter as it now is, rather then to try to rearrange its "original" parts for chronological consideration.

The Purposes of the Letter

(1) The letter informs the Philippians of Paul's present situation and his prospects for the future (1:12-26; 2:24).

(2) It thanks the Philippians for their gift (1:5; 4:10-20).

(3) It insures a good reception for Epaphroditus, who was returning with the letter (2:25-30).

(4) It prepares the way for the coming of Timothy (2:19-23).

(5) It assists the Philippians in solving certain problems in the church: persecution by opponents (probably Gentiles and Jews, and possibly legalistic or Gnostic Christians) (1:28-30; 3:2-19); dissension among members (1:27; 2:2-3; 4:2-3)—and helps them move on toward Christian maturity (3:12-21).

Philippians 1:1-11

Introduction to These Verses

Writings from prison often have a peculiar potency and glow. Some of them have influenced the course of human history for good or ill.

One thinks of the diabolical impact of Hitler's prison-begun *Mein Kampf* and the 700 vitriolic letters from the federal penitentiary in Atlanta written by Eugene Dennis, the general secretary of the American Communist party.

On the good side are John Bunyan's *Pilgrim's Progress* from the Bedford jail in England, Dietrich Bonhoeffer's letters, essays, poems, and prayers from a Nazi prison, and Olin Stockwell's *Meditations from a Prison Cell,* originally written on the margins of his Bible during his confinement in China by the Communists.

Anwar Sadat, the Egyptian leader, once said, "There are two places where you always find yourself—one is prison and the other is war." A prison experience gives a person time to think and often deepens and accelerates the convictions that are brought into a prison cell.

Paul's letter to the Philippians possesses an unearthly radiance. It is his most joyful letter. Through the centuries it has helped millions of people triumph over whatever circumstances have dashed their dreams. They have affirmed with Paul, *I can do all things in him who strengthens me* (4:13 NRSV).

Here is an outline of Philippians 1:1-11.

I. The Greeting (1:1-2)
II. The Thanksgiving and Prayer (1:3-11)

The Greeting (1:1-2)

Ancient Near Eastern letters normally began with the writer's name, the recipient's name, and the greeting (see Ezra 7:12; Daniel 4:1; Acts 15:23; and the many letters of the Greek world in Paul's time).

Paul altered the threefold form in several ways: by changing the Greek word *greeting* to *grace*, by joining to it the Hebrew word *peace*, by indicating the source of grace and peace, by adding comments about his authority, and even by commenting on the nature of his gospel (Romans 1:1-7; Galatians 1:1-5). He thus turned a rather commonplace opening greeting into a theologically rich initial benediction. God and Jesus Christ (Jesus the Messiah) are looking on the church with undeserved favor (*grace*), and bringing wholeness and well-being (*peace*) to their special people. May the church at Philippi recognize and appreciate its fortunate status!

That Timothy is included here with Paul (1:1) is probably due to several facts. Timothy was with Paul at the time of the founding of the church at Philippi (Acts 16:3-12). He therefore was known to the Philippians (however, only as a minor member of the team). He was to be sent soon to Philippi to check on the situation there (Philippians 2:19), and needed enhanced authority to deal properly with the church's problems (2:20-22). And Paul wanted to indicate at the outset of the letter that he gladly shared with Timothy authority in the church—that he himself was an example of the non-grasping humblemindedness he expected of the Philippians (2:3-8).

The evidence for this last point is that Paul applies both to himself and to Timothy the term *servants* (actually *slaves of Christ Jesus*. Only here among the opening greetings of Paul's letters does he share authority as

Christ's messenger with another person. When he includes other names (even Timothy) as senders of a letter, he regularly refers to them/him as *brothers* (NIV; NRSV = *members of God's family*) or *brother* (1 Corinthians 1:1; 2 Corinthians 1:1; Galatians 1:2; Colossians 1:1; Philemon 1). He usually reserves for himself unique authority. But here even the first verse of Philippians is shaped to introduce one of the main emphases of the letter.

Servants (*slaves*) indicates those who belong totally to another, who are subject utterly to the will of another. In Paul's and Timothy's case they are in bondage to *Christ* (that is, the Messiah) *Jesus*, the exalted *Lord* (master); see 2:9-11.

The saints in Christ Jesus are God's people who by virtue of their union with the Messiah Jesus are set apart from the evil people of the world to be God's peculiar possession. They are becoming like God in character and activity. The term *saint* implies for Paul no particular degree of spiritual-moral excellence. He even calls the woefully imperfect Corinthians saints (1 Corinthians 6:1, 2; 16:15). They are saints because they belong to God, not because they are morally perfect.

The *bishops* (NRSv; NIV = *overseers*) *and deacons* may be two kinds of church officers at Philippi, or they may be two ways of speaking of one group, the elders who presided over the church (Acts 14:23; 15:2, 6; 20:17; Titus 1:5). The problem in deciding which is meant is that in Greek the word usually translated *and* can also be rendered *even*. Thus the meaning here might be, "the overseers who serve."

If two groups are meant by Paul, the overseers are administrators of the spiritual and material affairs of the Christian community. The deacons would be their assistants in serving the needs of the poor, the sick, and the imprisoned. If one group is meant (the elders, who are overseers who serve), Paul at the outset of his letter means to stress the elders' servant role along with his own (1:1) and Christ's (2:7). It may be that the elders thought of themselves and their position more highly than they ought to have thought (2:3-4).

The Thanksgiving and Prayer (1:3-11)

Paul follows the standard form in Greek letters of the time. Their writers sought in various ways to secure at the beginning of letters the goodwill of the readers by thanking God or the gods for good things known about the readers and/or good things that had happened to the senders, and by indicating interest in the recipients' welfare (health and property) through references to prayer in their behalf.

Here Paul is thankful for several things. He begins with a joyful recollection of them, particularly of their *partnership* (NIV; NRSV = *sharing*) *in the gospel from the first day until now* (1:5). *Partnership*, sharing together in something, also translated *participation in, partakers with, fellowship of, sharing,* and *contribution,* is a word much beloved by Paul. He uses it thirteen out of the nineteen times it appears in the New Testament, and he uses it in various forms several times here in Philippians (1:5, 7; 2:1; 3:10; 4:15).

Christians are called to share in the life of God's Son (1 Corinthians 1:9), in the blood and body of Christ (1 Corinthians 10:16), and in his sufferings (Philippians 3:10). They share in the Spirit (2 Corinthians 13:14; Philippians 2:1), in the grace of God (Philippians 1:7), in the work of the gospel (Philippians 1:5), and in contributions to less fortunate Christians (Romans 15:26; 2 Corinthians 8:4; 9:13). For Paul, sharing comprises the essence of the gospel, of Christian experience, and of Christian activity.

By the Philippians' partnership in the gospel, Paul quite clearly has in mind, among other things, the gift brought to him by Epaphroditus (4:14-18).

Paul is thankful also for the certainty he has that God is at work in the life of the Philippians (1:6). God is present both in their ongoing support of the gospel through their gifts, and in the perfecting of personal character (love, knowledge, discernment, purity, righteousness—1:9-11). This certainty gives him confidence that they will be prepared for *the day of Jesus Christ*, that is, the day of judgment (2 Corinthians 5:10).

A third item for which Paul expresses thanks to God is the Philippians' sharing with Paul in God's *grace*. By this grace Paul is strengthened in his imprisonment and in his *defense and confirmation of the gospel* (1:7). Grace here is more than God's unmerited favor that leads to salvation; it is God's particular help in a time of weakness and need (2 Corinthians 12:9), in this case his imprisonment. The Philippians are so much partners with Paul that they are wearing the same chains he wears and standing with him when he defends and confirms the gospel. Before writing this letter Paul undoubtedly had had a hearing before some judge or judges (at Ephesus? at Rome? at Caesarea?), and was awaiting the outcome (2:23). In all of these experiences, he says, I know you are standing with me. Therefore, *I have you in my heart* (NIV; NRSV = "You hold me"). *They are indeed partners* with him, and he is thankful to God for them.

The nature and content of Paul's prayer for the Philippians, as evidenced here, are worthy of comment. As to its nature, it is very personal (note *I, my,* and *mine* in 1:3, 4, 9). It is continuous (1:4), inclusive (*all of you,* 1:4—Paul has no favorites at Philippi), and joyful (1:4).

His prayers for them contain thanksgiving (see above) and petition for several blessings: ever-increasing love; knowledge and discernment, without which abounding love may be directed to the wrong ends; moral purity (the Greek word suggests ability to stand examination in the light of the sun) and blamelessness (not stumbling or causing others to stumble); and the fruits that come from a right relationship with God in Jesus Christ (see Galatians 5:22-23). Paul wants them to be able to stand judgment at *the day of Christ Jesus* (1:6, 10).

The thanksgiving and prayer are so warmly personal and charged with loving emotion that the criticisms Paul later directs toward the Philippians in this letter (1:27–2:4, 14; chapter 3; 4:2-3) would have no sharp sting.

§ § § § § § §

The Message of Philippians 1:1-11

§ The opening of this letter is warmly personal and gracious. From almost the first line the Philippians would feel both the graciousness of Paul and the grace and peace of God.

§ In the first words Paul's humble sharing of authority in God's service with Timothy and his inclusion of the whole church, with its bishops and deacons, as God's servant people along with Timothy and himself, strikes a democratic and familial note.

§ Paul's thankful remembrance of them, in particular for their generous support of his mission, his confidence in them and their future as the special people of God, his tender yearning for them, and his desire to enrich their lives with knowledge and spiritual fruits, all say eloquently *I have you in my heart* (1:7 NIV; NRSV = *you hold me . . .*) and *I yearn for you all with the affection of Christ Jesus* (1:8).

§ Paul was a master psychologist. Whenever he could, he accentuated the positive and minimized the negative. He knew that praise and encouragement accomplished more with new Christians than stinging criticism. *Sharing* was not just a work with him, but a total attitude and way of life. Paul shared and wished his converts to share with him because God shared the gift of the Son.

§ § § § § § §

Philippians 1:12-26

Introduction to These Verses

From the greeting, the thanksgiving, and the prayer Paul turns to the message he wishes to convey to the Philippians (to "the body" of the letter; see the outline on pages 4-6).

During his imprisonment Paul obviously had been meditating on the effects of his circumstances on the progress of his mission of spreading the gospel in the world. Had his chains put fetters on that gospel? Quite the contrary! (See also 2 Timothy 2:9.) He saw evidence that the gospel was marching on precisely because of his imprisonment.

Undergirding his confidence was his firm belief that *in everything God works for good with those who love him, who are called according to his purpose* (Romans 8:28). Paul was overwhelmingly certain that he had been divinely called to spread knowledge of God and the gift of Jesus, the Messiah, everywhere (Acts 26:15-18; Romans 1:1-6; 15:15-16; 2 Corinthians 2:14-16; Ephesians 3:1-13; Colossians 1:24-29). The message contained in the "good news" was: *In Christ God was reconciling the world to himself* (2 Corinthians 5:19). As Christ's ambassador Paul's task was to invite the world to be reconciled to God (2 Corinthians 5:20).

Chains could not defeat God's purpose. Nothing but faithlessness on the part of the ambassador(s) could hinder that purpose (1 Corinthians 4:1-5; 2 Corinthians

4:2; 6:3-10; Philippians 3:12-16). Indeed, suffering was central to being a disciple of Jesus (Matthew 10:16-23; Mark 8:24; Acts 14:22; Romans 8:17). By suffering the ambassadors were toughened, purged, encouraged (Romans 5:3-5), humbled and empowered (2 Corinthians 12:7-10), and made more effective as witnesses (2 Corinthians 4:7-12). Therefore, disciples of Jesus should rejoice in their sufferings (Romans 5:3; 2 Corinthians 12:9; Philippians 4:4; Colossians 1:24; 1 Thessalonians 5:16-18).

This section has three parts.
I. Paul's Imprisonment (1:12-14)
II. Paul's Christian Opponents (1:15-18)
III. The Coming Verdict (1:19-26)

Paul's Imprisonment (1:12-14)

In Philippians 1:12-26 Paul rejoices that what has happened to him has advanced the gospel in two respects. First, it has made clear at the highest political levels (see below) that Paul is a prisoner because he is a representative of Jesus, the Messiah, not because he is guilty of any political crime or civil wrongdoing. Second, what has happened to Paul has inspired other Christians to proclaim the Christian message without fear of consequences (1:12-14).

What Paul means in verse 13 by the word *praetorian* (NRSV = *imperial guard*; NIV = *palace guard*) is disputed. It may mean *praetorian guard*, or it may refer to the emperor's or governor's palace. If Philippians was written from Rome, Paul probably would mean the emperor's large and elite bodyguard, several members of which may have guarded Paul in shifts in his own home in Rome (Acts 28:16). If the place of writing was Ephesus or Caesarea, the word could refer to the king's or governor's palace (Mark 15:16; John 18:28, 33; Acts 23:35).

Everyone else may refer to non-soldiers outside the

guard quarters or palace, such as lawyers and court personnel, who were involved in the disposition of Paul's case. It could hardly mean the whole city outside.

Paul's major point is that it is known at the highest levels that his only offense is the proclamation of the gospel. He does not suggest here that converts to Christ are being made among highly placed Romans. But he certainly implies that it is to the advantage of his mission that his service of Christ is recognized and being talked about at the center of Roman life and power.

The second positive result of what has happened to Paul (verse 12), as noted above, is that many of the brethren have been encouraged to proclaim the Christian gospel more courageously than before Paul's imprisonment. Paul's fortitude has lit a fire to theirs!

Paul's Christian Opponents (1:15-18)

In verses 15-18 Paul mentions some who preach Christ but are envious of and hostile to Paul (verse 14). Exactly who these people were and why Paul mentions them here is not clear. An answer depends in part on the place of Paul's imprisonment.

If he was at Rome, the spirit of *envy and rivalry* (verse 15) and hostility to Paul (verse 17) finds a fairly simple explanation. Paul had not founded the church at Rome. It may have been begun by visitors from Rome who were converted in Jerusalem at Pentecost (Acts 2:10), or by Christians scattered after the martyrdom of Stephen (Acts 11:19-20).

The Roman church had its own leadership and program of education and evangelism. Yet Paul claimed authority over it and over the whole Gentile church, since he regarded himself as God's priest for the Gentile world (Romans 15:15-16). This claim may have been rejected by the Roman church (and perhaps by other churches not founded by Paul). The Roman leaders may well have felt that they were as God-called and as spirit-endowed as Paul. They may have denied that Christianity's future was bound up with what would happen to Paul, that his claim that *I am put here* [by God] *for the defense of the gospel* (Philippians 1:16) was presumptuous. They even may have believed he had brought on himself his own troubles, perhaps by foolhardy actions, and that Christianity could move on quite adequately without him.

Since the preachers proclaim Christ (verse 17) and Paul even rejoices in their proclamation of Christ (verse 18), it is evident that they were not preaching heretical doctrines. They were only hostile to Paul. Paul then mentions these Roman rivals to the Philippian church to warn against any such divisiveness at Philippi. We know that the spirit of rivalry (power-grabbing) was present there (Philippians 1:27; 2:2-4; 4:2-3).

If Paul was at Ephesus or at Caesarea when he wrote Philippians, we must assume the existence there of a partisan spirit, revolving around various leaders, such as Paul addressed at Corinth after his departure (1 Corinthians 1:10–4:21).

More important to us than the exact identity of the rivals is the magnificent triumph of Paul's spirit over the painful slight we learn about here. *What then?* means "What does it matter?" Christ is being exalted and promoted, whether my unique apostleship is recognized or not; and in that I *rejoice* (verse 18). Only by divine grace can we rise above personal rejection and insult.

The Coming Verdict (1:19-26)

Next, Paul proceeds to show how the coming verdict in the trial will advance the gospel. He contemplates the consequences of life or death.

Deliverance here (verse 19) is the regular Greek word in the New Testament for *salvation*, and may mean either present health and well-being or ultimate salvation (usually the latter in Paul's letters).

Scholars are divided on the meaning of the word in this passage. If Paul intended the present sense, he meant that he felt sure of his vindication in the coming trial, a conviction also recorded in 1:25-26 and 2:24. But he may have meant the salvation beyond death (eschatological salvation), as may be indicated by the fact that the words *will turn out for my deliverance* are an exact quotation from Job 13:16 in the Septuagint version. There Job has in mind vindication before the heavenly, not an earthly, court. Paul's later phrase, *to die is gain* (NIV; NRSV = *dying is gain*)(verse 21), clearly suggests he was thinking in part about ultimate vindication and approval. Clearly he did not know how the trial would turn out, though he hoped for a favorable verdict.

Two sources of strength in his agonizing uncertainty and waiting are buoying him up: the knowledge that the Philippians are praying for him, and the help given by *the Spirit of Jesus Christ* (that is, the Holy Spirit; the Holy Spirit and Christ are equated by Paul in Romans 8:9 and Galatians 4:6). On the Holy Spirit's help in times of trouble, see Mark 13:11; Luke 12:11-12.

Honoring Christ *by life or by death* is possible because the Christian is forever under the lordship of Christ. As Paul puts it in Romans, *Whether we live or whether we die, we are the Lord's* (14:8). Death changes only the area of service.

The high point of this section is verse 21: *For to me to live is Christ, and to die is gain.*

In the Greek text *to me* is emphatic, really meaning "the way I look at it." *To live is Christ* may have both a mystical and an ethical meaning. To go on living is to be in union with Christ—he in me and I in him—and to have the blessedness this union brings. To go on living is to serve Christ and to glorify him by *fruitful labor* (verse 22).

To die is gain, from Paul's perspective, is well explained in 2 Corinthians 5:1-10. There he contrasts our impermanent, tent-like existence on earth with the coming, eternal, building-like existence in heaven—in an order prepared by God, not by humans. Through death we are *changed* into a heavenly body like Jesus received by the Resurrection (1 Corinthians 15:35-50; 2 Corinthians 4:14). In the new age *we will be with the Lord forever* (1 Thessalonians 4:17). We shall possess *an eternal weight* [abundance] *of glory beyond all comparison* (2 Corinthians 4:17). This prospect draws Paul on.

Hence, he knows not what to choose for himself—life or death (Philippians 1:22). But when he thinks of the Philippians, he knows that continued life in the present body would be better for them—for their *progress and joy in the faith* (verse 25). He hopes to visit them again (1:26; 2:24). Then they will have opportunity to boast of what Christ Jesus has done for Paul (1:26).

§ § § § § § §

The Message of Philippians 1:12-26

This section of Philippians is rich in meaning for us today. § From every human point of view Paul's imprisonment was a disaster. It involved personal humiliation and suffering, delay of his plans for evangelizing the West, inconvenience and probably great expense for his associates and for himself, embarrassment for the church before the Jewish and Roman worlds, and much more.

§ But by meditation, prayer, and the Holy Spirit's illumination Paul saw not the discouraging negatives of his situation but the heartening positives—all rooted in his conviction that God has a way of bringing good out of evil. He saw Christ's suffering and death as a glory road that he himself was privileged to walk in imitation of his Lord. He speaks later in this letter about his sharing of Christ's sufferings as if it were a splendid station on the path to resurrection life (3:10-11).

§ Equally striking is his magnanimous attitude toward the ungrateful and hostile Christian preachers who increased the bitterness of his prison experience. Slight and insult are not commonly known to be inspirers of joy and rejoicing. Where did Paul learn this response if not from Jesus (Matthew 5:11-12)?

§ Finally, Paul's calm in the face of death and his loving concern at this time for his much more fortunate readers reveal a source of power not of this world. The text here discloses the agony of his soul in his awful predicament and that he is fully human. He wants the prayers of the Philippians and the Holy Spirit's help (1:19). But he is in no doubt about the outcome: *Christ will be exalted in my body, whether by life or by death* (1:20).

§ § § § § § §

Philippians 1:27–2:11

Introduction to These Chapters

Up to this point in the letter Paul has been talking
mostly about himself—his gratitude toward and love for
the Philippians, the content of his prayer for them, how
the gospel is being advanced through his imprisonment,
the attitudes of Christian leaders toward what has
happened to him, and the struggle within him as he faces
the coming verdict. The personal pronoun *I* has been
prominent.

At 1:27 the pronouns become *you* and *your*.
Introspection becomes instruction and exhortation. His
readers have heard enough about him. He now wants to
talk about them: their problems and needs, their
attitudes, their opponents, their recent doings, and their
responsibilities as citizens of two orders at once (as
Christians in the Roman colony at Philippi and as
members of the heavenly *community*—1:27; 3:20). The
concern about *you* continues all the way to 4:9. The letter
ends (except for the final greetings and benediction) with
a section centering on *you and I* (4:10-20).

This section has two parts.
I. The Threats to Unity (1:27–2:4)
II. Jesus Christ as Source and Pattern (2:5-11)

The Threats to Unity (1:27–2:4)

In this passage Paul discusses life in the church at
Philippi under the metaphor of good citizenship. In the

city-states of the Greco-Roman world, good citizenship involved a high degree of cooperative attitude and effort at all levels of life. Philosophers and teachers of ethics believed that free people could achieve a high degree of perfection in individual and social life, if they would work together. Factionalism and party spirit were a constant threat to democratic living.

In verse 27 the change from *me* to *you* is abrupt. In a sweeping summary he calls the Philippians to a manner of life appropriate to citizenship in two orders of existence: in the church and in the heavenly commonwealth.

The Greek word behind *live your life* (v. 27, NRSV) literally means *to conduct oneself as a citizen* (so NIV). The Philippians were proud of their status as a Roman colony and their privileges and responsibilities under Roman law. Paul appeals to that pride here and exhorts them to act appropriately and responsibly in their life as citizens. If they do, they will show themselves worthy of the gospel of Christ.

This life of good citizenship embraces several attitudes and activities.

First mentioned here is living in unity (having *one spirit, with one mind, striving side by side.* (NRSV; NIV = *contending as one man*) *One spirit* may refer to the Holy Spirit, to the human spirit, or to the human spirit as controlled by the Holy Spirit—probably the last. What Paul wants is mutuality, interdependence, cooperation, and harmony.

Second here is an emphasis on contending together for *the faith of the gospel* (verse 27). This phrase apparently refers to the faith that has resulted from the preaching of the good news about Jesus Christ. That Jesus, the Messiah, was God's way of salvation to all who believe, was under attack by both unbelieving Jews and scoffing Gentiles (1 Corinthians 1:20-25). The Philippians should contend vigorously for this true understanding of God's work in the world.

Third here is courage in the face of danger and in the midst of suffering (1:28-30). Since Paul says that they and he are engaged in the same *struggle* with opponents, we can identify who the Philippians' opponents were: unbelieving Jews, who stressed salvation by obedience to the law (3:2-3); false teachers in the church (3:18-19); and Gentiles incited by Jews against Christians.

Paul attempts to bolster the courage of the Philippians by several supports: the certain coming destruction of these enemies and the salvation of the faithful (at the coming of Christ?); the privilege of suffering *for the sake of Christ*; and the knowledge that they and Paul are suffering in the same cause.

Noteworthy in verses 27-30 are the metaphors Paul uses to convey his exhortation. His readers are told to conduct themselves like good citizens, to stand firm like courageous soldiers repelling an attack, and to strive together as in an athletic contest. The Greek word behind *frightened* (NIV; NRSV = *intimidated*) here (verse 28) is a colorful one. It was occasionally used for the shying of a startled horse. They are not to be stampeded by their enemies.

The fourth attitude and activity in the life of good citizenship mentioned here is selfless devotion to the welfare of others (altruism). This is set forth in one of the most profound passages in all of Paul's letters (2:1-11). He sees in Christ Jesus the supreme illustration of other-mindedness and the effective cure for disunity.

The passage starts out with a repeated call to unity and harmony in the church at Philippi. In verses 27-30 of chapter 1, Paul dealt mostly with the threat from enemies outside the church and the church's need for togetherness in facing this threat. Now he looks at the selfishness and conceit inside the church—as great a danger to its well-being as that posed by external foes.

The four phrases of 2:1 in the Greek text have no verbs, are vague, and are hard to relate to the progress of thought. In this text the *if* expresses not doubt, but rather the truth of what is being said. In English, *since* would be more accurate than *if* here. Or if the *if* is to be kept, we should translate as follows: "If, as is the case, there is any. . . ."

But difficulties still remain. Whose encouragement? Whose love? Whose participation? Whose affection and sympathy? Is it Paul who has given these to the Philippians through introducing them to life in Christ and in the Holy Spirit? Or is all of this from God and Christ, with no reference to Paul here at all? Or are both Paul and divine sources referred to? Probably the last. The meaning would then be: If you have received benefits from God through me (encouragement, love, life in the Holy Spirit, affection, and sympathy), make me fully happy by going on to complete harmony of mind and life.

The chief obstacles to this oneness are selfishness and conceit—counting oneself better than others (verse 3). This attitude should be reversed. Christian humility requires putting others first and being concerned about others' interests ahead of one's own. Christian fellowship overcomes the spirit of selfishness that says "mine," "yours," "his," and "hers." "Ours" is the possessive pronoun that Christian fellowship knows (Acts 2:42-47; Romans 15:26).

In 2:5 Paul seems to exhort the Philippians to follow the example of Jesus Christ and have among themselves the unselfish and humble attitude toward others that he has.

However, some scholars dispute this interpretation and maintain that Jesus Christ is presented here not as an ethical example to be followed, but (together with the church as his body) as the source from which and the realm in which the life of otherness, humility, and unity is experienced. Some other translations make Christ an example here, whereas the NRSV and others suggest the other interpretation.

The problem of meaning arises because in the Greek text there is no verb in the second half of verse 5. It has only, "which also in Christ Jesus." One might supply here either the verb "was" or "you have." Thus the meaning intended by Paul could be, "Let your bearing towards one another arise out of your life in Christ and the church."

The two meanings are not necessarily mutually exclusive. It is quite possible to understand the verse as offering the Philippians in Christ Jesus both a source and an example of Christian thinking and acting in relation to others.

Jesus Christ as Source and Pattern (2:5-11)

How did Jesus Christ relate to God and others in attitude and deed so that he became the source and pattern of Christian thought and conduct?

The explanation comes in what most scholars believe is an early Christian hymn in honor of Christ Jesus (2:5-11). This passage seems to have rhythm and strophes (stanzas), though scholars do not agree on the exact number and content of the strophes. It is printed in poetic form in some translations.

We do not know whether the hymn was composed by Paul, by someone associated with him, or quite independently of him in some section of the early church. Whether Paul wrote it or not, he obviously agreed with its view of Jesus Christ and included it in his letter because it says about Jesus what he wanted the Philippians to know about their Lord's attitude (toward himself, toward God, toward others) and his redemptive activity.

The hymn traces Christ's thought and work from his glorious pre-incarnate existence and self-emptying to his earthly experience of humble servitude, and to his subsequent exaltation by God to universal lordship. It stresses the voluntary character of Jesus Christ's self-abnegation, and implies that God rewards those who follow Jesus Christ in renouncing and self-seeking and in acting for the benefit of others.

Some phrases of the hymn deserve special comment.

(1) *Though he was in the form* (NRSV; NIV = *very nature,* but cf. footnote) *of God* (verse 6) is subject to various interpretations: that he shared in the divine essence or the divine mode of being; that he shared in the divine glory (John 17:5); or that he bore the image of God, as Adam did (Genesis 1:26-27; 2 Corinthians 4:4; Colossians 1:15).

The phrase does not say flatly that Christ was God—the New Testament normally refers to Jesus Christ as God's Son (Matthew 11:27; John 3:16; Romans 1:3; Galatians 4:4; Hebrews 1:2)—but it implies participation in God's being, attributes, and work, on the analogy of a human son to a father (John 5:17-20; 8:29).

Paul and the early church drew on Jewish and Hellenistic concepts concerning the word of God, the wisdom of God, and the Son of man to emphasize Christ's intimate relationship with God in Creation, redemption, and consummation.

(2) *Something to be grasped* (NIV; NRSV = *explained* verse 6) translates an obscure Greek word that appears only here in the New Testament. It can be understood in two senses in this passage: something not yet possessed but desirable and thus a thing to be grasped at; or something already possessed and thus a thing to be clutched and held onto.

Probably the first meaning is best here. Christ as Son (word, wisdom, man of heaven [Son of man], last Adam), participating in God's very being, attributes, and work, did not seek to wrest sovereignty over the universe from the Father in an act of rebellion. To grasp at sovereignty would be to make himself independent of the Father, instead of the obedient instrument of his redemptive purpose.

(3) *But emptied himself* (NRSV; NIV = *made himself nothing* verse 7) cannot mean that he gave up his identity as God's Son, but rather possibly his prerogatives as God's Son (omniscience, omnipresence, and glory). Or perhaps the phrase simply means that he poured himself out (for others)—he impoverished himself—instead of seeking to enrich himself. Thus the thought would agree with Paul's statement in
2 Corinthians 8:9: *You know the grace of Our Lord Jesus Christ, that though he was rich, yet for your sake he became poor, so that you through his poverty might become rich (NIV).*

(4) In the phrase *form of a*, as in verse 6, means full participation in the being, status, and activities of another, here a slave. In pouring himself out the heavenly Christ became one of us.

We are not told what he became a slave to, but it must mean to those things in an evil world that hold human beings in bondage: human limitations, death, sin, the law (Romans 6–7), and possibly the evil spirit-beings of which Paul speaks (Romans 8:38-39; Galatians 4:8-9; Colossians 2:15). He could not come into this world without coming under the forces that operate here. This does not mean, however, that he yielded to the pressure of those forces (2 Corinthians 5:21; Hebrews 4:15; 1 John 3:5).

(5) *In human likeness* (verse 7) probably stresses the full humanity of Jesus and means that he was fully like us in his basic constitution and his situation.

Whether the passage means that Jesus took our fallen nature has been much debated. In Romans 8:3 Paul says that God sent *his own Son in the likeness of sinful flesh* (NRSV; NIV = *man*). Did Paul distinguish between perfect, unfallen flesh and sin-dominated flesh and hold that Christ came in the former but not the latter? Possibly so, as some scholars maintain. Others argue that *likeness* means identity, and say that Christ took the same fallen nature that we ourselves have, and that he remained sinless because he constantly overcame the temptation to sin. New Testament writers stress the complete humanity of Jesus (Luke 2:52; Galatians 4:4; Hebrews 2:17; 4:15; 5:7-9; 1 John 4:2).

(6) *Obedient to death, even death on a cross* (verse 8) expresses the depth to which Christ's self-abnegating attitude and activity brought him. Death on a cross was undoubtedly the most shameful of deaths in Paul's time; it was reserved for slaves, criminals, foreign rebels, and the like.

Why Jesus' death was necessary is not indicated here. Paul deals with that elsewhere (Romans 3:24-26; 2 Corinthians 5:18-21; Galatians 3:13-14). Some scholars argue that Paul's reference to the *servant* (slave) here is an echo of Isaiah 52:13–53:12, with its teaching about the vicarious, atoning death of the servant of the Lord. But there is no hint of this here.

(7) *God has exalted him* (verse 9) indicates that God rewarded him who poured himself out for others. (In the theology of Paul and the church the exaltation was believed to have occurred through God's act in Jesus' resurrection and ascension—Acts 2:32-33; Romans 1:4). Paul and the church knew that Jesus had taught that *whoever humbles himself will be exalted* (by God) (Matthew 23:12; Luke 14:11; 18:14) and that this is a principle of God's kingdom. And the implication is strong here that the Philippians who abase themselves and exalt others will likewise be blessed by God.

The reward *given to* Christ—the Greek word suggests a gift of grace—consisted of several elements:

(a) super-exaltation (the literal meaning of the Greek word behind *exalted*), that is, elevation to the highest possible degree of status and authority, possibly meaning higher than he had before his self-emptying;

(b) *the name that is above every name*, that is, *Lord* (meaning the Master, borne also by God in the Old Testament), who is elevated above all so-called gods, lords, principalities, and powers (1 Corinthians 8:5-6; Ephesians 1:20-21; Colossians 2:15) and who possesses *all authority in heaven and on earth* (Matthew 28:18; 1 Corinthians 15:24-25);

(c) the worship of creation in its totality (heaven, earth, underworld) and the universal confession of the lordship of Jesus Christ (see Revelation 5:13), a worship and confession that bring glory (honor, praise) to God the Father—the ultimate authority (1 Corinthians 15:28) who exalted the Son as the instrument of divine redemption.

§ § § § § § §

The Message of Philippians 1:27–2:11

§ The appeal to the Philippians for humble service of others, rather than self-aggrandizement, is powerfully reinforced by this magnificent hymn about the attitude and actions of the church's Lord.

§ The hymn and the appeal for unity that introduces it glorify what to the Greek mind was largely despised: humility. Philosophers and the highborn regarded humility as servility, and thought it appropriate only for slaves and lower-class people. It was not a virtue to be cultivated. Humility was viewed quite differently by Jews and Christians, as we know from the Old Testament, the Qumran texts (the Dead Sea Scrolls), and the New Testament.

In Jewish and Christian thought humility is the attitude one should have in the presence of almighty God and God's messengers. To be proud is to be guilty of sin, for it puts self above the honor and obedience due to God and the covenant law. Many persons glory in their wisdom, might, and riches, when they should glory in their understanding of and relationship with God and in their doing what God delights in (Jeremiah 9:23-24).

Jesus condemned every sort of pride and exalted the humility of children. He washed the feet of his disciples and enjoined them to do likewise—and even to become the servant (slave) of all (Mark 10:42-44).

Nothing could glorify humility and self-abnegation more than this hymn, written or cited by Paul, about the self-emptying of Christ in behalf of others. Beside it in grandeur is a shorter companion piece about Christ's becoming poor so that we might be made rich (2 Corinthians 8:9).

§ § § § § § §

Philippians 2:12-30

Introduction to These Verses

After presenting Christ Jesus as the unselfish, other-minded, self-emptying, obedient, and highly exalted One who became the source and example of the Christian spirit and life, Paul turns to the Philippians' situation in the light of Christ's work. This short section has only two parts.

I. The Philippians' Mission (2:12-18)
II. God's Helpful Servants (2:19-30)

Paul points out that as Jesus Christ was obedient to the purpose of God through his obedience *unto death* (2:8), so the Philippians must be obedient—both to Paul and to God's purpose for them (2:12-13). Then Paul returns to thinking about the outcome of his trial and its possible effect on the Philippians.

First he thinks theologically about their situation in the light of his death or survival (2:12-18). Then he thinks in practical terms about their specific needs and what possible help his associates may be able to offer them (2:19-30).

The Philippians' Mission (2:12-18)

While musing theologically on the Philippians' situation, it seems that Paul was struck by the parallel between it and that of the children of Israel in the wilderness. Paul had earlier compared the church at Corinth with the disobedient and grumbling Israelites under Moses (1 Corinthians 10:1-10). While the Philippians, unlike the Corinthians, *have always obeyed* (verse 12), there are still problems to be dealt with in the church at Philippi, and their obedience is therefore not complete. Note the *much more* here.

To fear of their outside opponents (1:28-30), to *selfishness, conceit,* and contentiousness (2:2-3; 4:2-3), other problems may be added: probably some complaining (NIV; NRSV = *murmuring or arguing* (verse 14), maybe some yielding to the enticements of *a crooked and depraved* (NIV; NRSV = *perverse*) *generation* around them (verse 15), and possibly some libertine conduct on the part of certain individuals within the church (3:19).

In thinking about these dangers, Paul may have compared himself with Moses and, like Moses, sought to warn his followers in a farewell appeal. Such appeals by departing patriarchs and religious leaders, modeled after those of Moses in Deuteronomy 34 and Jacob in Genesis 49, were common in Jewish literature of Paul's time. That he was meditating on Moses and Deuteronomy may be suggested by the fact that here in verse 15 he quotes Deuteronomy 32:5 (from the Septuagint version, with some changes). The *much more in my absence* of verse 12 may mean "my absence in prison" or it may mean "after my death."

His admonition to *work out your own salvation,* if separated from the following *for God is at work in you* would be a betrayal of Paul's own doctrine of salvation by faith alone. When the two are kept together we have the proper Pauline balance: God works in us and we must cooperate by pressing on toward perfection of life (Philippians 3:12-16) and by making our faith become active in deeds of love (Galatians 5:6, 13-14; 6:1-2, 10).

By *salvation,* Paul is not thinking so much of individual salvation as the salvation of the whole church, though, of course, both are involved. Heretofore he has been addressing the entire church. Purely individual salvation would be inappropriate after the exhortation in 2:1-11 for *all* to have the mind of Christ. And the word *salvation* can have the meaning of well-being or health in a present sense, as well as in a future sense (eternal life). The meaning then would be: By obedience to me (whether I am present or absent), by God's power at work in you, and by constant diligence on your part, you can fulfill God's good purpose for you of total health and well-being (now and future).

Fear and trembling is used frequently by Paul, but not with regard to one's attitude before God. More often it refers to one's attitude toward others and people in authority (see 1 Corinthians 2:3; 2 Corinthians 7:15; Ephesians 6:5). Here it means reverence, awe, or a deep and genuine respect for one another.

Complaining (NIV; NRSV = murmuring) or arguing (verse 14) was characteristic of Israel's unbelieving attitudes in the wilderness (see Exodus 16:7; Numbers 11:1; 1 Corinthians 10:10). At Philippi they were probably directed from one person toward another, and perhaps toward their leaders (*bishops and deacons,* 1:1). These attitudes, Paul implies, bring criticism on the church and compromise its witness in the world around it.

Christians are called to a life beyond reproach. Outsiders are not impressed if they simply see in Christians the kind of attitudes and acts they know in their society. As faultless children of God, Jesus' followers will shine *like stars.* Jesus had this goal for his disciples, though for him it was the light of a hilltop city and a lamp stand (Matthew 5:14-16).

The Philippians are not just to illuminate the sins of the *people* around them by shedding light, but they are to help dispel the darkness by *holding fast* to or *holding out* (the Greek can mean either) *the word of life* (meaning the gospel that brings life). By holding fast to the apostolic gospel, they will hold out the truth that saves.

Their fidelity to the gospel will make Paul proud of his

ministry at the *day of Christ*, that is, the day of Christ's judgment (2 Corinthians 5:10; 2 Thessalonians 1:6-10). At that time Paul will give an account of his stewardship (1 Corinthians 4:1-5). The fidelity and final victory of the Philippians will show that Paul's life work was not for nothing. Be faithful not only for your own sake, he says, but also for mine!

His final comments in this section (verses 17 and 18) concern the effect of his possible death. He does not know how the trial will turn out (2:23). Through the imagery of sacrifice he seems to be saying that his death would be a libation added to the sacrifice to God offered up by the Philippians themselves.

Paul considered Christian life and service a sacrifice to God (Romans 12:1). Even the gifts sent by the Philippians to him in prison were *a sacrifice acceptable and pleasing to God* (Philippians 4:18). Paul knew that in the Temple at Jerusalem a libation of wine or olive oil was poured out over a sacrifice or beside it. So Paul's death as a libation would add to the Philippians' offering of faith and life, and make their sacrifice complete and fully acceptable to God. His death, then, would not be meaningless, but would cause them both to rejoice over it. Paul refused to see defeat in anything that happened to him or to the life of a Christian (Romans 8:28).

God's Helpful Servants (2:19-30)

Paul now turns to practical matters about the Philippian situation. The Philippians need help, but Paul can't help them in person until the trial is over. Anxious about them, he wants to hear good news about them, probably especially about their response to this letter that Epaphroditus is to take (see below). So he plans to send Timothy soon, but not before there is some indication as to how the trial will turn out (verse 23).

Several remarks about Timothy serve to build up Timothy's stature with the Philippians. As noted earlier,

Timothy was only a minor member of the team at the time of the founding of the church at Philippi. Now he is to be Paul's official representative in looking after their interests.

First Paul says that he is his soul-companion, his confidant. *I have no one like him* in the Greek text is really, "I have no one like-minded" or "of equal soul" (probably meaning *with me*). He is Paul's *alter ego* and will think about the Philippians and act in relation to them as Paul himself would.

Then he says that Timothy is completely unselfish and utterly dedicated to Jesus Christ's cause, unlike some other self-centered people around Paul. Timothy will be genuinely concerned about the Philippians' welfare. Paul does not say who the selfish Christians were, and it is futile to guess. It is possible that Paul, not wanting to part with Timothy, had pressed on several others the request to represent him at Philippi but had been turned down for what Paul regarded as inadequate reasons. Thus the disappointed tone here.

Finally, by calling Timothy his *son* (the Greek has *child*) who *served with me* (literally, "worked as a slave with me") in the proclamation of the gospel, Paul indicates that Timothy is no mediocre substitute for himself. Timothy has already proven his worth to Paul and to the Philippians (verse 22). According to Acts 19:22 and 20:3-6, Timothy had been in Philippi twice since the founding visit.

Timothy was an example of the other-mindedness that Paul was asking for. He was supremely qualified to show the Philippians what having the mind of Christ would require them to be and do.

The second exemplary person whom the Philippian church should honor (verse 29) was Epaphroditus. It was he who had brought the Philippians' gifts to Paul (4:18) and who apparently had intended to remain with him to serve as needed. Paul may have known him before this trip; *my brother and fellow worker and fellow soldier* implies more than a short contact with him.

At some point in his mission to Paul he fell seriously ill, even close to death. Quite likely it was on his way to Paul's place of imprisonment (Rome, Ephesus, or Caesarea). Word was carried back to Philippi by someone, perhaps a traveler in the other direction, concerning his illness. The result was that the Philippians were deeply concerned about him and the success of his mission.

He made it to Paul with the gifts, but under the circumstances Paul thought it best for him not to remain to try to serve as the Philippians' representative. Undoubtedly out of consideration for his health, his homesickness (verse 26), his family, the worried church at Philippi (verses 26, 28), and the extra strain on Paul over the care of an incapacitated associate in the city where he was imprisoned (*that I may be less anxious*—verse 28), Paul decided to send him home and to have him carry this letter with him.

Paul must have felt that Epaphroditus would be criticized by some for bungling his mission. Therefore, he made it emphatically clear that Epaphroditus had done his absolute best, even risking his life to discharge his service as the Philippians' messenger and minister (verse 25) to Paul's need. Epaphroditus too was an illustration of the kind of otherness and self-sacrifice Jesus Christ and Timothy exhibited and the Philippians should emulate.

§ § § § § § §

The Message of Philippians 2:12-30

§ Paul saw the remedy for the Philippians'
shortcomings as being a cooperative working of the
Philippians and God: *Work out your own salvation . . . for
God is at work in you* (2:12-13).

The first *work*—in the phrase *for God is at
work*—translates a different Greek word, and means "for
God continually and mightily energizes you." God is the
Great Energizer, with whom the Christian is to cooperate
in the achieving of God's good purpose of salvation.

§ The passage does not teach the sole efficacy of divine
grace and human passivity or the efficacy of human work
with God's assistance. The Christian is to work because
God has been and is working mightily (in Jesus Christ)
for human redemption (see John 5:17). Thus Paul,
Timothy, and Epaphroditus are *fellow workers* and
servants (1:22; 2:16, 22, 25, 30). The Philippians' task is to
labor side-by-side with Paul in the gospel (4:3), and to
work continually toward the present and future
well-being of the Christian community. Then they will
shine brightly as *stars*, holding fast the word of life
(2:15-16).

§ § § § § § §

Philippians 3

Introduction to This Chapter

One major threat to the church is yet to be considered: false teaching about the way of salvation, advocated by *enemies of the cross of Christ* (3:18).

If this letter to the Philippians is a unity and not a composite of several letters illogically put together after Paul's time, we must say that Paul's transition to the subject of this pressing danger is very abrupt.

This chapter may be outlined as follows.
  I. Introduction (3:1)
 II. The True Way to Righteousness (3:2-21)
    A. Renunciation of assets (3:2-8)
    B. Faith-identification with Christ (3:9-11)
    C. Progressing in Christ (3:12-16)
    D. Following models (3:17-21)

Introduction (3:1)

Verse 1 is a puzzle. The Greek work translated *finally* or *in conclusion* sometimes introduces the end of a letter (as in 2 Corinthians 13:11). Or it can serve as a transitional word to a new subject and mean simply, "Well then" or "Now." Which did Paul mean here? Did he intend to conclude the letter and then suddenly think of something else important to say? Or was he simply shifting over to a new subject? Probably the latter.

The Greek word (*chairete*) translated *rejoice* or *be joyful* was also a common form of greeting in Paul's time, meaning *hail, farewell,* or *goodbye.* It certainly means the latter in 2 Corinthians 13:11, but hardly so in Philippians 1:18; 2:17, 18, 28; 4:4, 10. The presumption is that it means *rejoice* in 3:1, especially since *in the Lord* is added, echoing a phrase used in the Psalms (see 32:11; 33:1). To rejoice in the Lord, for Paul, means that Christ is the source, object, and sphere of rejoicing.

In the second half of 3:1 *the same things* that Paul does not mind repeating may refer to his many references to rejoicing. He may be saying that, if rejoicing is practiced by the Philippians, it will help keep them safe from the dangers that threaten them. Or the statement may introduce what follows by saying he is now *writing* what he has said before orally to the Philippians. Or again it is possible that he is referring to what he has written in previous letters. Many interpretations of this puzzling statement have been offered by scholars.

The False Teachers

Paul now launches into a strenuous warning against certain teachers who are trying to mislead the Philippians. He says three things about them.

(1) He calls them *dogs, evil-workers,* (NRSV; NIV = *men who do evil*) and *those who mutilate the flesh. Dogs* was a term of contempt by which Jews described Gentiles who ate foods considered by Jews to be unclean. The context shows that Gentiles cannot be meant. Thus Paul is hurling back on people of a Jewish point of view one of their own derogatory terms. *Those who mutilate the flesh*—in Greek, "the mutilation," or "the cutters"—is a contemptuous reference to circumcisers, who are evildoers. As he goes on to show, they insist on doing what God does not require for righteousness.

(2) They put *confidence in the flesh. Confidence* is dependence on or trust in someone or something. *The flesh* is that which is human, what people are capable of

being and doing without reference to God, here human privilege and achievement. These teachers regard human privilege and achievement as *gain* before God (verse 7).

(3) They are *enemies of the cross of Christ* (verse 18). *Their god is their stomach, and their glories in their shame,* with minds set on earthly things (verse 19). Some scholars have taken the devotion to the belly here to refer to scrupulous attention to what goes into the stomach (food laws), the *shame* to be the shame of circumcision in which they glory, and the *earthly things* as values that pass away. More likely, however, Paul is referring to some kind of libertines who indulge the belly (gluttony), revel in sexual and other freedoms, and are altogether earthbound in their satisfactions and goals.

Exactly who these opponents were has been long debated. There are basically three views:

(1) They were Jews, Pharisees like Paul was, who gloried in their heredity, ancestral religious rites (including circumcision), zeal for the law, and standing before God. They actively opposed Paul's preaching of salvation through the cross of Christ and sought to nullify his work in Macedonia and elsewhere (Acts 17:5-9; 18:12-17).

(2) They were Jewish-Christian missionaries, perhaps from Jerusalem. In opposition to Paul, they sought to fasten the law on Gentile Christians as a requirement for membership in the Christian church. Paul opposed such Christians in his letter to the Galatians.

(3) They were Jewish-Christian Gnostics ("Divine Men;" see the Glossary), the same group Paul opposed in 2 Corinthians 10–13. They considered circumcision the badge of membership in the true Israel (the church); claimed special charismatic powers; believed they already enjoyed, through their spiritual rebirth, the full blessings of the kingdom of God (there would be no future resurrection of the evil body); and thought themselves free to do as they liked in the realm of

personal morality. They claimed perfection of life, and regarded the suffering of Paul and his associates as evidence that they had not reached the perfection they themselves had attained. They were self-seeking (lived off the gospel) and were excessively proud. They were the very antithesis of the other-regarding, self-emptying Christ and his faithful servants Paul, Timothy, and Epaphroditus.

Recent scholarship has turned increasingly toward the third view as best explaining the central emphases of Paul's letter to the Philippians.

The True Way to Righteousness (3:2-21)

If their way to righteousness (salvation) is wrong, what is the true way, as Paul conceives it? The whole of chapter 3 deals with this question.

Renunciation of Assets (3:2-8)

Paul's assets, utterly renounced as giving him credit before God, were (1) assets from national background and heredity, and (2) assets from personal choice and achievement.

In the first group are: proper Jewish childhood circumcision (on the eighth day); privileged national and tribal origin (from the divinely chosen people of Israel and the esteemed tribe of Benjamin); pure Hebrew blood and upbringing in untainted Hebrew culture (the Greek text reads "a Hebrew of Hebrews").

In the second group are: membership in the Pharisaic party (a party honored for conscientious and detailed obedience to the Mosaic law); zealous activity in that sect in upholding the law (by persecution of lawless Christians); and faultless personal performance of the law's requirements for right living.

These striking assets led Paul to put *confidence in the flesh*, that is, in his human privileges and achievements. Such confidence gave him a righteousness (rightness) of his own making (verse 9), a self-righteousness (Romans 10:1-3). It did not put him in right relationship with God. Such a relationship cannot come by human performance of the commands of the law, he says, however good that performance may be.

In fact, as he points out in Romans and Galatians, the more one studies the law and seeks to become righteous by it the more one comes under the power of the sin that operates through it and becomes subject to the death that sin brings (Romans 7:5, 10-11). The law promotes sin by negative stimulation: by making a person want to do what the law forbids. The law's only function is to make sin recognizable (Romans 3:20; 5:13; 7:7) and to point to the Savior (Galatians 3:22-24), who alone has power to defeat sin and put one in right relationship with God. Thus human assets and human effort are worthless.

Faith-Identification with Christ (3:9-11)

Human assets, as a ground of acceptance with God, must be jettisoned if one is to come to *know* Christ. For Paul and the biblical writers in general, to know God or Christ involves much more than to have knowledge *about* God or Christ. It means to be in intimate, humble, adoring, and obedient relation to them. The word is used, for example, of the intimate relationship of marriage (Genesis 4:1; Matthew 1:25). Thus personal, experiential knowledge is meant here.

According to the present passage, to *know* Christ means to be *found in him* and thus to have his righteousness (the rightness he has before God) at the day of judgment. It also means to experience the power he wields by virtue of his resurrection, to share his sufferings (both in his death on the cross and in the sufferings of the church as his body), and to have the blessed hope of ultimate resurrection from the dead (meaning, from among the physically dead). Present Christian experience, while a foretaste of the final life in the kingdom of God, is not the full realization of redemption, as the false teachers held.

Faith in Christ (verse 9) is complete surrender to and personal trust in Christ, not trust in one's assets and achievements. It is the response of the whole self to the God who is presented in Jesus Christ.

Progressing in Christ (3:12-16)

The false teachers seem to have believed that they became perfect at the time of their baptismal birth in Christ. They maintained that they were enjoying now the fullness of the life of the kingdom of God. Nothing more was to be expected. Paul refutes this vehemently.

Knowing Christ is an ongoing experience, he says. Perfect life in Christ is not achievable in this life, but only at the transformation to be experienced at the coming of Christ (3:20-21). Paul continues to speak in the first person, using himself as an example of what he means. Like a runner in a race, I forget what lies behind me (my assets from heredity and achievements, my sins and failures, and my attainments as a Christian) and continually press on, *straining* to reach the goal-marker and to obtain the prize at the end of the race.

What the prize is Paul does not say. Is the prize God's call to come up and inherit the Kingdom? Is the prize full knowledge of Christ, of which Paul has had a growing but incomplete experience? Is it resurrection life (verse 11) with Christ? Probably all of these. Second Corinthians 5:1-10 shows the prize to be an eternal new order of incomparable glory, made by God and not by human hands, where we shall be clothed with a new body and be *at home with the Lord* (2 Corinthians 5:8).

Following Models (3:17-21)

Paul knows that teaching is not enough. Truth must be embodied in life if it is to have compelling power. In chapter 2 he gave the Philippians teaching (2:1-4). And then he offered them models to follow: Christ and Timothy and Epaphroditus.

The Philippians can be helped on in the true way of salvation if they pay attention to heaven-oriented, not earth-minded, leaders: Paul and those whose lives are patterned after his. Earth-minded leaders will lead them into libertine indulgence and final destruction.

We should not set our minds on earthly things, Paul says, because our *citizenship* (our homeland) is in heaven. Our life while here should be in keeping with what we are and with our destiny. That destiny will be realized when our Savior, the Lord Jesus Christ, will come from heaven to transform our bodies (that is, our persons) by his unlimited power into his own glorious likeness.

§ § § § § § §

The Message of Philippians 3

§ Assets from heredity and personal achievements, if trusted in for salvation, are a hindrance to God's favor and blessings. As Paul pointed out so bluntly in his letter to the Galatians, salvation is by faith alone. The bringer of that salvation is Jesus Christ, *who gave himself for our sins to rescue* (NIV; NRSV = *set us free*) *us from the present evil age* (Galatians 1:4). *A man is not justified by works of the law but through faith in Jesus Christ* (Galatians 2:16 NRSV). *Self-righteousness* comes through human assets and works but not God's righteousness (that is, a right relationship with God).

§ If this is so, then all modern religions of achievement must be ineffective. This includes those forms of Protestantism that stress salvation through education and becoming through doing.

§ Important also is Paul's position that being *in Christ* during this life brings with it no absolute perfection. We *press on* in the knowledge that that goal is yet to be reached. We are Christians in the making, ever seeking to become actually that which we became ideally at the point of beginning.

§ § § § § § §

PART SIX Philippians 4

Introduction to This Chapter

The letter concludes with some specific counsels, some general exhortations, and an extended word of thanks for the gift the Philippians sent at the hands of Epaphroditus.

Paul has dealt in chapters 2 and 3, on theological and personal grounds, with the serious threats to the health of the Philippian church, arising from the nefarious teaching of the "Divine Men." But some manifestations of the problem still remain, and Paul seeks to deal with these.

Chapter 4 has four parts.
   I. Introduction (4:1)
  II. Quarrel in the Philippian Church (4:2-9)
 III. Thanks for the Philippians' Generosity (4:10-20)
 IV. Concluding Greetings and Benediction (4:21-23)

Introduction (4:1)

Paul's transition from the theoretical to the practical in verse 1 is noteworthy. As he does so often in his letters, Paul speaks tenderly, lovingly, and positively to his readers before he criticizes them. Note the words *my brothers*, (NRSV; NIV = *dear friends*) *whom I love and long for, my joy and crown* and *my beloved*. He knows that discipline is effective only if it is administered in the context of love, here even yearning love out of the pain of separation. In this spirit of love he exhorts them to *stand firm . . . in the Lord.*

My joy and crown puts together two of Paul's great words. *Joy* is a key word of Philippians (1:4, 25; 2:2, 29; 4:1). It comes from the same Greek root as the word *rejoice* (1:18; 2:17; 4:4, 10). The whole letter bubbles over with joy.

Crown (*stephanos*) here is not a king's diadem, but rather the victor's laurel wreath given by judges to the winner at the Olympian games (see 1 Corinthians 9:25). The Philippians, successful in their struggle against enemies, will comprise Paul's *crown* at the judgment day (2:16; 3:20-21).

Quarrel in the Philippian Church (4:2-9)

The selfishness, conceit, rivalry, grumbling, and questioning that, according to 2:1-14, marred the life of the Philippian church apparently had its center in a dispute between two women: Euodia and Syntyche. Paul appeals to each woman individually (*to agree with each other* (NIV; NRSV = *to be of the same mind*) *in the Lord.* He wants them to have the same attitude that the Christ who emptied himself had and that Paul, Timothy, and Epaphroditus have exhibited. If one is really *in the Lord,* no other attitude is possible.

Paul does not mention the cause of the quarrel. It seems to have been a power struggle, perhaps between two charter members (Acts 16:13). We can speculate that the bishops and deacons (Philippians 1:1) were unable or unwilling to cope with the quarrel, possibly because they themselves were caught up in the struggle. Rival factions would inevitably spring from the kind of theology advocated by the "Divine Men."

Paul has three specific suggestions for overcoming the problem.

(1) The phrase *in the Lord* points to the hymn of 2:5-11,

and suggests that both women take another look at the attitude and action of their Lord.

(2) They are to accept the help of Paul's *loyal yokefellow*, (NIV; NRSV = *companion*) some person or persons of stature among them—known to them but not to us—who can act as peacemaker. Modern scholars have made attempts at identification: Timothy, Epaphroditus, Luke, Silas, Syzygos (the Greek word behind *yokefellow*, taken as a proper name), or the whole church (regarded as yoked to Paul). If the yokefellow was an individual person, he had Paul's mind and approach (as *true* implies).

(3) These women are to realize what they have been and are. They have been Paul's, Clement's (a person unknown to us), and other workers' companions in evangelizing. Thus what they are doing now is not typical of them. And their names, along with the others, are in *the book of life* (they share a common destiny; Revelation 3:5; 13:8; 17:8).

But, more generally, the best antidote is to rejoice continually in the Lord. Dissension cannot exist when there is mutual rejoicing. This mutuality will have its effect on the surrounding world. People outside will see your *gentleness* (better translated *magnanimity*—the opposite of insisting on one's rights.

Another powerful motivation to unity is the fact of the Lord's nearness (verse 5). *The Lord is near* may mean that he is near to help (in the Holy spirit), or that his final coming is close at hand, or both. In any case, it means that the Philippian church need not and must not continue in its present condition. It stands under the grace and judgment of the Lord.

By constant trust, prayer, and thanksgiving, God's marvelous peace (well-being, wholeness), available to those who are in Christ Jesus (that is, in union with him and his church), will keep them safe and well in their innermost being.

A second general counsel directed toward the health and stability of the church is offered in verses 8 and 9. It concerns the members' thinking and acting.

They are to let their minds dwell on the best and the most highly-regarded virtues of their own cultural heritage. The virtues Paul lists here (what is *true, honorable,* (NRSV; NIV = *noble*) *just,* (NRSV; NIV = *right*) *pure, pleasing,* (NRSV; NIV = lovely), *commendable* (NRSV; NIV = *admirable*) were emphasized by philosophers, particularly by the Stoics, in Paul's time. There is nothing here that is distinctively Christian, although all are in harmony with Christian ethical teaching. Paul seems to be saying, Let your minds dwell on all that you were taught to believe is best in life. He recognized that we become what we dwell on in our thinking.

Then, they are to keep Paul's teaching, preaching, personal example, and traditional church standards ever before them. They are to shape their actions according to what they have *learned, received* (the Greek word suggests, from church tradition), *heard,* and *seen in me* (Paul's life before them). New Christians, especially, need examples of what discipleship of Jesus Christ really means. Paul did not shrink from this responsibility and applied it to others as well (2:19-30; 3:17).

If they think and do what is right, the God who brings *peace* will be with them to assure stability of life and ultimate salvation.

Thanks for the Philippians' Generosity (4:10-20)

At the end of the letter Paul discusses what was one of its main purposes: to express thanks to the Philippians for being concerned about him and sending him Epaphroditus with some gifts (verse 18). These gifts were alluded to twice before in the letter (see 1:5; 2:25-30). However, no adequate thanks had been expressed for them, though appreciation for Epaphroditus's service to him (2:30) and comradeship in ministry (2:25) had been offered.

Paul's remarks about the gifts reveal some embarrassment in regard to them. He writes guardedly, as if he might say the wrong things. He doesn't want to express gratitude too profusely, lest they think him in greater need than is the case and feel sorry that they did not help him sooner.

Paul wants to minimize the importance of earthly things so that they will know that he puts spiritual blessings ahead of material ones and has divine help in his predicament. He wants to assure them that he can get along with very little, so they will not think him to be dependent continually on their benefactions.

He knows also that the Philippians gave liberally to the collection for the Jerusalem church when they could not afford to do so (2 Corinthians 8:1-3); and he is embarrassed that they have felt the necessity now of helping him. Taking money, not once but several times (Philippians 4:15-16), from friends who cannot afford to give it is difficult. But to reject it altogether would be inconsiderate and offensive.

Above all, by accepting the gifts he is violating the principle of entire self-support (1 Corinthians 9:15-18; 2 Corinthians 11:7-11) he had adopted with all the rest of his churches. No wonder he threads his way carefully through this last section of this letter. He says so little by way of actual thanks for the gifts that some scholars have called this section "the thankless thanks."

Several points in his thanks for the gifts are worth noting.

(1) He thanks them more for their concern than for their gifts (verses 10, 14, 17). By this he says, "I want you and your love more than your money" (see 2 Corinthians 12:14). Paul refused to allow the force of his gospel and its call to acceptance and radical obedience to be blunted

by suspicion of his hearers that he was really after what they had in their pockets (1 Corinthians 9:16-18).

(2) The Philippians' gifts to him are really sacrifices *pleasing to God* (verse 18). Here, in language drawn from the Old Testament (Genesis 8:21; Exodus 29:18) and used by him in Ephesians 5:2 with reference to Christ, he makes the point that gifts to God's servants are in actuality gifts well-pleasing to God.

(3) Reliance on God *who strengthens me* and contentment with one's circumstances, whatever they are, is the proper Christian attitude. Paul accepted with joy what came from God's hand, as this remarkable letter has shown throughout.

(4) God-reliance and self-reliance are desirable characteristics of Christian ministry. Paul makes it abundantly clear that, while he accepts the Philippians' gifts (verses 15-16), he prefers independence and self-sufficiency and wishes no more help from them. He practically writes a receipt for what they have sent him (*I have received full payment and more*) and adds, *I am filled.* "Thanks, but no more!"

(5) He is as interested—or more—in the benefit to the Philippians of their giving to him. In God's economy the gift blesses the giver (verses 17, 19). God will see to it that their needs (the Macedonian churches were poor— 2 Corinthians 8:1-2) will be met, in Christ Jesus, out of his glorious abundance.

Concluding Greetings and Benediction (4:21-23)

On the meaning of *saints*, see the commentary on 1:1-2. On the reference to *Caesar's household* (NIV; NRSV = *the emperor's*), see page 10.

§ § § § § § §

The Message of Philippians 4

Both the theological and the practical dimensions of this letter attest to the versatility of its author. One moment we are *in the heavenly places*, thinking God's and Christ's thoughts after them (2:5-11); next we are on the earth amid the hassle of contending theologies about the way of salvation (3:2-21). Then we move on to a squabble between two women who apparently were grasping for power in the church. Finally we encounter a sticky problem about how to say thank you for gifts that must be acknowledged but basically are not wanted.

Theologians—and Paul was a masterful one—are not supposed to be practical persons. But here in Philippians is a remarkable blend of theology and ethics, undergirded with sound psychology about how to handle difficult people and situations. Paul knew not only how to raise up churches but how to care for them as well, as would a *nurse* and a *father* (1 Thessalonians 2:7, 11). Paul's patience with his stumbling and often obnoxious Christian children rivaled that of Moses in the wilderness.

In 4:21-23 there are many jewels, such as: the suggestions for healing divisions within the church, especially the emphases on rejoicing, magnanimity, trust in the Lord, prayer, and thanksgiving; the importance of keeping one's mind on the best values and one's eyes on the finest examples of Christian living; the lesson that contentment in one's situation, no matter how desperate it is, comes from complete trust in the one who gives power to do all things; that generosity to others does not go unnoticed by the God who wants to supply all our needs; and that God's goal for us is *peace* (health, well-being), now and hereafter.

§ § § § § § §

Introduction to Colossians

The Church at Colossae

From the fifth century B.C., Colossae (in the Lycus River valley of central Asia Minor, some 100 miles east of Ephesus) was a populous wool-working and cloth-dyeing center. It lay near the cities of Hierapolis and Laodicea. The three cities, all prosperous, vied with one another in the textile and wool-dyeing industry. They are mentioned together in Colossians 4:13.

The church at Colossae was founded by Epaphras (1:7). He was a Colossian (4:12), who may have been converted by Paul during his long ministry at Ephesus (Acts 19:10) and who represented Paul (1:7) in the evangelization of the three cities of the Lycus valley (4:12-13). Epaphras was in prison with Paul at the time of the writing of this letter (Philemon 23). He was the source of Paul's information about the situation in the church at Colossae (1:8).

Philemon, Paul's convert (Philemon 19)—also probably at Ephesus—was the owner of the slave Onesimus (Philemon 15; Colossians 4:9). Philemon was a prominent member of the church at Colossae. His house was large enough to accommodate the meetings of the Christian church (Philemon 2) and to have a guest room for Paul (Philemon 22). By addressing the letter to Philemon also to the church in your house (verse 2), Paul made sure that the whole assembled congregation would hear the letter and take to heart what he had to say about the proper Christian reception, both by his owner and the whole church, of a converted runaway slave.

Paul's Purpose in Writing to the Colossians

Paul had never been to Colossae (1:4, 9), but he felt a responsibility for the church there. Not only had a convert of his founded the church, probably under his direction (1:7), but he knew himself to be God's apostle and priest to the whole Gentile world (Romans 15:16; Colossians 1:24-29). The church at Colossae lay in his special area of evangelization (Romans 15:19-20; 2 Corinthians 10:13-18). Undoubtedly, when Epaphras described its needs to Paul, he resolved to help by writing this letter.

Several purposes are apparent.

(1) Some people, whether members of the church or not, were advocating a *philosophy and empty deceit* (2:8 (NRSV; NIV = *hollow and deceptive philosophy*). This attitude threatened to undermine the truth about Jesus Christ long preached by the church, and the way of salvation taught by Paul. Paul was deeply concerned that the church not be turned in a false direction and be subverted both doctrinally and ethically. He wanted it to *lead a life worthy of the Lord, fully pleasing to him, as you bear fruit in every good work and as you grow in the knowledge of God* (1:10 NRSV).

The philosophy involved the worship of angelic, cosmic powers (2:8, 18, 20) in addition to Christ. These were celestial spirits, who apparently were regarded as God's agents in governing the movements of the heavenly bodies. Thus the spirits in some respects controlled human destiny, as astrological thought holds. Their worshipers observed feast days, special seasons, and certain practices to honor and perhaps appease these spirits (2:16-23).

Apparently it was taught that all these powers, along

PHILIPPIANS–2 THESSALONIANS

with Christ, constituted God's fullness, that is, the full range of God's attributes and manifestations. Allegiance to Christ was not enough to guarantee salvation. The ruling powers also had to be recognized and pacified.

This philosophy stressed special visions offering secret knowledge of ultimate reality and the way of salvation. Paul thought that such knowledge led to pretensions and self-congratulation (2:18).

The heresy seems to have been a mixture of elements from several sources: Judaism (perhaps like that found in the Dead Sea Scrolls); early Gnosticism (like that advocated by the "Divine Men"); and Hellenistic astrology and pagan mystery cults. Paul felt that glorifying and pacifying astral powers debased Christ and introduced practices that were a threat to Christian freedom.

(2) Paul meant by the letter to introduce Tychicus, the carrier of the letter, who was to encourage the Colossians in the true way of salvation and inform them about Paul's circumstances (4:7-8).

(3) He wished also to ensure a good reception for Onesimus, the converted runaway slave, who was returning in company with Tychicus to his master at Colossae (4:9).

(4) Epaphras, the founder of the church, apparently was under attack by the heretic philosophers and needed Paul's support. This letter would enhance his standing with the Colossian church (4:12-13).

(5) Paul meant to prepare the way for the visit of John Mark (4:10); and also to urge Archippus, possibly Philemon's son or a resident in Philemon's house (Philemon 1-2), to carry out faithfully some responsibility entrusted to him in the Lord's service (4:17). Since Epaphras was in prison with Paul, it may be that the service he was to perform was to carry on Epaphras's pastoral responsibilities.

(6) Finally, Paul seems to wish to establish his

authority and teaching firmly in the Gentile churches, both those founded directly by him and those raised up by his followers (1:7, 23-29; 4:16).

Authorship, Place, and Date

Two positions are widely held today on the question of authorship.

(1) Paul, as the letter clearly claims (1:1, 23; 4:18), was the author.

As was frequent with Paul (1 Corinthians 16:21; Galatians 6:11; Colossians 4:18; 2 Thessalonians 3:17), he added an authentication in his own handwriting.

In Colossians there is some variation in language, style, and theology from Paul's other letters, due to the special circumstances under which Colossians was written. But the similarities to the other letters are greater than the dissimilarities.

Furthermore, strong ties with the letter to Philemon, unquestionably written by Paul, argue for Paul's authorship of Colossians. The two letters have the same senders (Paul and Timothy), greetings from many of the same persons (Aristarchus, Mark, Epaphras, Luke, Demas), and the mention of Archippus. The letters seem to have been written at about the same time and carried to Colossae by Tychicus and Onesimus.

(2) A disciple of Paul wrote the letter to the Colossians in Paul's name.

Many facts argue that Paul was not the author. A few are: the use of many words not found elsewhere in Paul's letters; the absence of Paul's characteristic ideas (righteousness, justification by faith alone, the purpose and function of the law); the highly speculative view of Christ, especially in 1:15-20; and the strong emphasis on apostolic tradition as a way of counteracting heresy.

Possibly a disciple of Paul, who was thoroughly familiar with Paul's language and thoughts, used his master's authority as a way of meeting heresy sometime after Paul's death.

Since the case against Paul's authorship is not conclusive, the discussion of the letter here will assume the correctness of the letter's own claim.

If the letter was written by Paul, the place was Ephesus, Rome, or Caesarea. The date was about A.D. 55–62. If a disciple wrote it, the time was after Paul's death, possibly A.D. 70–90, and the place is unknown.

PART SEVEN Colossians 1:1-14

Introduction to These Verses

These verses are the letter's introduction. They may be outlined as follows.
  I. Greetings (1:1-2)
  II. Thanksgiving (1:3-8)
  III. The Prayer (1:9-14)

Greetings (1:1-2)

In Colossians the writers are characterized somewhat differently than in the opening words of the letter to the Philippians. There both were *servants* [slaves] *of Christ Jesus* for a particular reason. Here Paul is an *apostle* and Timothy is *our brother*, the way Paul begins some other letters when he includes another name along with his (1 and 2 Corinthians; see also Philemon).

When Paul feels no need to stress his authority, he simply lists the names of the senders without characterization (as in 1 and 2 Thessalonians). And frequently he names only himself as the sender and offers more or less impressive credentials (see Romans, Galatians, Ephesians, [1 and 2 Timothy, Titus]). Paul was sensitive to the situation in each church to which he was writing and adapted his opening greetings accordingly.

Paul speaks to the Colossian church as Christ Jesus' official ambassador. *Apostle* means literally *one sent forth*. It carries the meaning of a person authorized to be the official representative of the one sending him. Not only was Paul the official representative of Christ Jesus to the Gentile world (Romans 15:15-16; Colossians 1:27)—and thus to the Colossians—but he was that *by the will of God*. Therefore, the chain of authority ran from God to Christ Jesus to Paul. He had high credentials indeed for speaking to the Colossians about proper Christian doctrine and life, in view of the challenge from rival teachers.

Timothy (*a brother*, meaning *a fellow Christian*) was Paul's right-hand man, confidant, and emissary to Paul's churches (Philippians 2:19-22). Since he was from Lystra (Acts 16:1-3) in southern Galatia (the Roman province just to the east of Asia, where Colossae was located) and since he had been with Paul in Ephesus (Acts 19:22), he probably would have been known personally by Epaphras and through him, by word of mouth, to the Colossian church.

The church members at Colossae are called here *the saints* (NRSV; NIV = *holy*) and *faithful brothers in Christ*. The word *saints* means the people chosen and set apart as God's exclusive possession. *Faithful* here probably does not mean trustworthy or reliable (as in 1:7; 4:7, 9), but believing or having confident trust (as in Galatians 3:9; Ephesians 1:1), though both ideas may be intended by Paul. *Brothers in Christ* indicates that they are members of one family by union with Christ.

Thanksgiving (1:3-8)

This thanksgiving, a standard part of contemporary letters, comprises one long sentence in the Greek text. For clarity it is broken down into several sentences in English translations.

The *we* are Paul and Timothy and possibly other Christians who gather around Paul when we pray *for you*. That others had access to Paul when he was a prisoner is evident (Acts 28:16; Philippians 4:21-22; Colossians 4:7-14). Prescribed times of prayer were morning, noon, and evening, though Paul seems also to have prayed constantly (Romans 1:9; Colossians 1:9; 1 Thessalonians 1:2) and exhorted others to do so (1 Thessalonians 5:17).

Two reasons for their thanksgiving are given first: (1) *your faith* (trust), which you have because you are in Christ Jesus (that is, in him and the church, his body); and (2) *the love which you have for all the saints* (that is, your faith issuing in practical service of all in the Christian community—Galatians 5:6, 13; 6:2). Both of these (faith and love) are based on and motivated by *the hope laid up for you in heaven.*

Paul does not describe the content of the hope here. But we learn from 1:27 that the church's exalted Lord is himself the *hope of glory.* Though he is now in heaven and hidden from our view, when he is revealed (3:4) at his glorious coming, the Christians' well-guarded inheritance will be received from that Lord (1:12; 3:1-4, 24; 2 Corinthians 5:1-10). This Christ-centered hope, when preached, evokes faith; and faith becomes active in deeds of love.

The triad of faith, hope, and love occurs elsewhere in Paul's letters (see, for example, 1 Corinthians 13:13; 1 Thessalonians 5:8-10). Here in Colossians hope, rather than love or faith, seems to be basic and praised the most highly. Since the triad appears in parts of the New Testament not written by Paul (Hebrews 6:10-12; 1 Peter 1:3-8), it may have been a kind of summary of the Christian life in the early apostolic church, used flexibly and creatively by Paul and others.

The Colossians have already heard about this hope through Epaphras, Christ's and Paul's faithful representative, who preached God's true word (the gospel) to them. Paul is thankful that the gospel (about the *grace* [graciousness] *of God*—verse 6) has come to the Colossians. That is, the gospel is taking root, bearing fruit, and spreading in Colossae and indeed all over the world. Verse 10 shows that the fruit he has in mind here is *every good work.* The worldwide success of the preached gospel and its results give Paul and his associates a third reason (see 1 and 2 above) for joyful thanksgiving to God.

Paul implies here that this success is proof of the gospel's validity and that the Colossian Christians therefore should be wary of the philosophy and empty deceit (2:8) being spread by the false teachers.

The Prayer (1:9-14)

Paul mentions here three subjects of his and others' constant prayer.

(1) *Full understanding by the Colossians of God's will.* The passive form (called by scholars "the divine passive") in the Greek word translated here *be filled* was used by Jesus about 100 times in his sayings (see, for example, Matthew 5:4; Luke 12:7) to suggest God as the actor. So it is used here. It is God who imparts spiritual wisdom and understanding (1 Corinthians 2:10-16). Paul wants the Colossians to have knowledge of the spiritual level, but not the human kind (*an appearance of wisdom,* 2:23) the false teachers are parading.

(2) *A life worthy of the Lord, fully pleasing to him.* A full, spiritual knowledge of God's will leads to right conduct and action, the kind of a life the Lord approves and will approve at the day of judgment (2 Corinthians 5:8-10). Paul frequently speaks of pleasing God or Christ (Romans 8:8; 1 Corinthians 7:32; 2 Corinthians 5:9; 1 Thessalonians 4:1).

Pleasing God was an important concept in the Hellenistic Judaism of Paul's time and in the Dead Sea Scrolls. Paul gives it a Christian orientation by the statement that his life is to be *worthy of the Lord,* that is, suitably in agreement with the attitudes and actions of the Lord Jesus Christ (Philippians 2:5-11) and what he requires of his followers (Ephesians 4:1; Philippians 1:27).

The result of this kind of a life is the abundant fruit of good works and continual growth in the knowledge of

God. Paul held that, while we are not saved by our good works, the Christian is expected to produce the fruit of good works (Romans 2:6-11; 2 Corinthians 9:8; Galatians 5:6).

(3) *Strengthening with God's mighty power.* In the Greek text several synonyms for power are heaped up here to accent its magnitude (see also Ephesians 1:19-20). God's almighty power is adequate for all the needs of the Colossians, including the achieving of the kind of life that is pleasing to the Lord. It will be adequate for occasions where endurance (in the face of enemy attacks, such as those launched by the false teachers) and patience (in relation to one's own fellows) are needed. But it will not be simply Stoic endurance and patience. It will be endurance and patience undergirded by joyful thanksgiving for the wonderful inheritance the Father has qualified (or authorized) us to share in.

This inheritance consists of membership among God's holy people in the light-like Kingdom of God's beloved Son. This privilege is experienced now in foretaste through deliverance from the tyranny of darkness, where evil powers rule (Luke 22:53; Acts 26:18), and from the bondage and guilt of sin. That the Kingdom is both present and future in this passage is clearly evident: It is inheritance, laid up in heaven and hoped for (verses 5, 12) and to some degree realized now (note *he has rescued* and *we have redemption*, verses 13-14).

§ § § § § § §

The Message of Colossians 1:1-14

This introductory section has several important themes.
First we learn about Paul, Timothy, and Epaphras
and the gospel they preached and lived by. Paul had an
unshakable conviction that he stood in a chain of
command that reached through Jesus Christ to God.
Timothy and Epaphras were his Christian brothers and
fellow servants (slaves) in conveying to the Colossians
and indeed to the whole world the good news Paul had
received from God through Jesus Christ. Together they
thanked God for the Colossians and prayed continually
for their welfare and growth in Christian faith and
living.

They regarded the gospel they preached, about the
gracious purpose (will) of God to prepare a holy people
for membership in the present and future Kingdom by
forgiveness of sins and redemption from the bondage
of evil powers, as unshakable truth. They saw this
gospel as a fruit tree being planted, taking root, and
producing fruit (good works) everywhere—obvious
testimony to its validity. He (and they) could plainly
see that it was transforming persons, remaking homes,
lifting and ennobling life here, and forming the outpost
of the coming new order.

Second, we learn about the Colossians' response to the
hope the gospel held forth. Faith was evoked, and out of
it came the deeds of love in the community of believers, a
growing faith and love.

Third, we learn about the church's needs: for fuller
spiritual understanding of God's will for themselves
and the world, for help to live in a way pleasing to God
and befitting their relation to the Lord Jesus, for
abundant power to overcome their enemies within and
without the community of faith, and for an increased

sense of privilege in being qualified by God to be members of Christ's kingdom and enjoying its benefits now while awaiting its final coming.

§ § § § § § §

Colossians 1:15-23

Introduction to These Verses

This is the most important and the most difficult
passage in the entire letter to the Colossians. It is shaped
in technical language to counter the false teachers' view
of Christ.

These teachers held that Christ was one of the many
cosmic powers (spirits) who comprised God's
fullness—all of whom needed to be worshiped and
appeased. They did not believe about Christ what the
writer of 1 Timothy did when he wrote: *There is one
mediator between God and men, the man Christ Jesus, who
gave himself as a ransom for all* (1 Timothy 2:5-6 NIV). In
reducing the stature of Christ and his work by making
him only one of the many manifestations and agents of
God in Creation, in the ruling of the cosmos, and in
redemption of the world's people, they were robbing
Christ of his unique importance. And, they were
destroying the Christian faith.

This passage falls into two parts.
I. The Uniqueness of Christ (1:15-20)
II. Application to the Colossians (1:21-23)

The Uniqueness of Christ (1:15-20)

Most scholars agree that in verses 15-20 we have a
poetic, rather than a prose, piece about the uniqueness of
Christ in Creation and redemption. There is a rhythmical

quality to the piece, a certain balance and parallelism in the structure of the thought. The lines are gathered into strophes (stanzas); ancient poetic devices of several kinds are used (alliteration, antithesis, and chiasmus).

Because there are many words here not used elsewhere by Paul or rarely used by him, many scholars have suggested that Paul used a poem or a hymn written by someone else before him and adapted it to his purpose in this letter. Others have argued that Paul composed the piece himself, using language and ideas derived largely from others. Whatever the original authorship, structure, and literary history of the piece, it lies before us in all its richness and complexity and dares us to probe its depths. If Paul did not write it entirely in its present form, he obviously agreed with its sublime view of Christ.

Since there is today no scholarly agreement on the number of strophes (stanzas) it contains (from two to five have been suggested), the exact contents of each, and what is to be attributed to Paul and what to others before him, we shall take the piece as it lies now and draw from it some of its major affirmations about Christ.

(1) Christ is the unique manifestation of God (verse 15a). An *image* in the New Testament sense is a true representation of the original. Since Jesus Christ is God's Son (see Romans 5:10; Galatians 4:4), he is a genuine representation of the Father (2 Corinthians 4:4-6). Paul would agree with the author of the Gospel of John that whoever has seen Jesus has seen the Father as well (John 14:9).

Behind the idea of someone or something as the image of God are the figure of Adam (Genesis 1:26-27), the concept of wisdom (Proverbs 8:22; Wisdom of Solomon 7:26), the Hellenistic view of the *Logos* (the Word), and the ancient concept of the divine king as the image of the deity he worshiped and represented.

(2) Christ is prior to and supreme over all created things (verse 15b). *Firstborn* here does not mean the first

created of all created beings and things, since the
following words indicate that Christ was above the
created order and the agent through which Creation was
accomplished.

The Greek work behind *firstborn* was used in reference
to the relation of the *Logos* to God (in Philo) and in
regard to the Messiah (in Hellenistic-Jewish
interpretation of Psalm 89:27); and it is compatible with
Jewish speculation about wisdom. The word implies both
preexistence and superiority.

(3) He was God's agent in the creation of all beings
and things and is also Creation's goal (verse 16). In
Jewish speculation, wisdom was God's agent in Creation
(Proverbs 3:19; 8:27-31). In their thought about Christ,
Christians adopted Old Testament concepts and Jewish
(and even some Hellenistic) beliefs where appropriate
(John 1:1-5; 1 Corinthians 1:24; Colossians 2:3).

Since whatever principalities, powers, spirits, and
angels—good or bad—that exist in the universe owe their
existence to God's work in Christ, Christ is Lord over
these powers. He is not simply one of them, to be
worshiped along with others, as the false teachers
maintain.

Christ is Creation's goal in the sense that all things are
to be united in him at the last (see Ephesians 1:10).

(4) Christ is the bond that holds the universe together
(verse 17b). The orderliness, unity, and continuance of
the universe are not accidental but are due to the
sustaining activity of Christ. The philosophers of Paul's
time speculated on what holds the cosmos together. The
Spirit of God, the Word (*Logos*), and wisdom were
suggested. Here the preexistent Christ is made the
cohesive force. (See also Hebrews 1:3.)

(5) Christ is the head of the church, which is his body
(verse 18a). Paul frequently speaks of the church as the
body of Christ (Romans 12:4-5; 1 Corinthians 10:16-17;
12:12-13, 27). This concept may have come from the

church's communion service in which all shared in one loaf, which Jesus had declared to be his *body* (Mark 14:22; 1 Corinthians 10:16-17).

Here and in 2:19, however, Christ is called the *head* of the body (the church), as also in Ephesians 1:22-23 and 4:15-16. Paul's purpose in Colossians in designating Christ as the head and the body (the church) as subordinate to the head is probably to emphasize once more Christ's supremacy. He also wanted to strike again at the Colossian heresy that sought to downgrade Christ.

There would be overtones for the Colossians and the Ephesians in this reference to Christ as the head, since in some Hellenistic thought of the time Zeus or the *Logos* was the head of the cosmos (the body). This background would suggest Christ's rulership of the cosmos also.

(6) He is the beginning of the new creation (verse 18*b*). He is the *beginning* of the age to come, since he is the *firstborn from the dead.* Through his death and resurrection others may die and rise through him to the newness of life (1:22; 2:12-13; 3:1-3). He is the *first fruits*, guaranteeing the future resurrection of the dead (1 Corinthians 15:20, 23). Here too he shows his preeminence.

(7) The divine fullness in its totality dwelt in him (verse 19). The meaning here seems to be that Christ contains and represents all that God is—and *that* by God's choice.

The heretics thought that God consisted of many powers (aeons), distributed through the universe, and that together they comprised God's totality. Against this view Paul says that in Christ alone the totality of divine powers dwells. God was in Christ (2 Corinthians 5:19), not in some partial way (as the divine might be in many human beings), but in God's fullness.

The church took the popular word and concept of the time, *fullness*, and used it to express the conviction about the Lord's supremacy over all rivals.

(8) Christ, through his death on the cross, is the means of God's reconciliation of the whole universe (verse 20). Underlying this verse is the assumption that heaven and earth are rifted in a battle of cosmic powers. (See also Romans 8:38-39; Ephesians 1:20-23.) God has begun the establishment of peace and order by the subjugation of the *powers* (NIV; NRSV = *rulers*) *and authorities* in Christ's death on the cross (Colossians 2:14-15). Through his resurrection, Christ entered into his kingly rule. At the last day he will complete the subjugation of every rule and every authority and power (1 Corinthians 15:24-28; Philippians 2:9-11).

Application to the Colossians (1:21-23)

The Colossians (clearly of Gentile background) were once estranged from God, hostile to God, and doing evil deeds. (See also Ephesians 2:1-3.) But they are now saints *and faithful brothers* (1:2), of whose faith and love Paul has heard (1:4-5) and who have become members of the Kingdom of God's beloved Son (1:13-14). God reconciled them through Christ's death in his physical body (not his "mystical" body, the church). God wants them to be faultless and irreproachable at the judgment day (Romans 14:10-12). This result is contingent on their continuing steadfastly in the faith and hope in which they began when they responded to the gospel that was preached to them and to all the world.

§ § § § § § §

The Message of Colossians 1:15-23

This profound passage, set in lyrical form, places
before us the unique claim of the Christian faith: that we
know and experience God fully when we know, believe
in, and obey Jesus Christ and are members of his church.
This claim was offensive to many people in Paul's day, as
it still is to adherents of other religions.

Paul placed Jesus Christ at the very center of the
universe. Using the highest terms known in Jewish and
Hellenistic religious terminology, Paul and some of his
fellow Christians painted a cosmic Christ, who was God's
agent in the creation of the universe and in bringing into
being the new creation (the church). Since he had opened
the gate of life to them and was actually making the
universe a true cosmos out of the chaos it had become,
the highest language they knew seemed appropriate to
express their individual and corporate experience of the
new life he had brought.

The terms they used were those of the first century,
but the faith and experience they describe are common to
Christians of every century since.

Christians will always exhaust human language in the
attempt to describe what they have found in Jesus Christ.

§ § § § § § §

PART NINE

Colossians 1:24–2:5

Introduction to These Chapters

At the end of the preceding part (1:23), Paul commented about the universal outreach of the gospel. He noted in 1:6 that it was taking root and bearing fruit in the whole world. If Christ's significance is cosmic, then all people will have to be informed concerning his identity and work.

That the gospel had actually reached *every creature under heaven* (1:23) is, of course, an exaggeration. But that it had reached the great centers of the Roman Empire, was spreading out from them, and was being talked about everywhere (even in Caesar's household—Philippians 1:13; 4:22) was fully apparent to Paul.

The spreading of this gospel to the Gentile world was precisely the work God had given him to do (Romans 15:15-16; Galatians 1:16). The shift from *we* to *I* here indicates that Paul is now stressing his unique apostolic responsibility for this work. But in describing his role here he uses the word *servant* (literally, *deacon*, meaning anyone engaged in service of any sort). Such a term would include Timothy (Philippians 1:1), Epaphras (Colossians 1:7). Tychicus (Colossians 4:7), Apollos (1 Corinthians 3:5), and others (2 Corinthians 11:23). These people were on a common footing in the work of evangelism. Paul had both a unique ministry and a shared ministry.

This section has two main parts.

I. Ministry of Suffering and Proclamation (1:24-29)
II. Paul's Concern for the Colossians (2:1-5)

Ministry of Suffering and Proclamation (1:24-29)

That Paul should be suffering for the sake of the Colossians (verse 24) might seem a strange statement to them. They did not know Paul personally, or he them. If the statement had been made about the imprisoned Epaphras (Philemon 23), the hard-working founder of their church (Colossians 4:12-13), they might have understood that Epaphras's suffering was for their sake. But Paul? By pointing out that Epaphras was his designated representative (1:7), Paul indicates his personal involvement in the Colossian situation, his authority over the church (verse 25), and the fact of his own sufferings in their behalf. He clearly hopes thereby to stimulate loyalty to himself and his gospel.

The purpose of Paul's sufferings—suggested in verses 25-29 to be sufferings connected with his apostolic labors—is put in cryptic language: *in my flesh I am completing what is lacking in Christ's afflictions for the sake of his body, that is, the church. (NRSV)* Many interpretations of this obscure statement have been made.

Did Paul believe that something was lacking in the redemptive adequacy of Christ's sufferings on the cross, and that this lack could be supplied by Paul himself? Hardly, because Paul regarded the death of Jesus as completely effective for salvation, once and for all (2:11-12; Romans 3:21-26; Galatians 3:13-14).

Did he believe that what was lacking was the *availability* of the benefits of Christ's afflictions and that he could do something about that? Such a lack is clearly suggested in verses 25-29. But how would this constitute a lack in the afflictions of Christ? Yet if Christ and his followers were one body (one reality), Christ's work would not be complete until theirs had been done, namely, the arduous and suffering-filled mission of getting the gospel out to the ends of the earth.

Did Paul have in mind here the common Jewish idea that there is a quota of sufferings that the messianic community must undergo before the end of the present age and the coming of the new age? Such suffering before the end is suggested in Mark 13:8 (and parallels in Matthew 24:6; Luke 21:9).

Did Paul think that his sufferings were helping to fill up this quota, reducing the number of sufferings his churches would have to bear, and thus hastening the coming of the end? So many modern scholars believe.

Perhaps the answer lies in a combination of these last two suggestions. Paul clearly foresaw a bad time for himself and for Christians before the end (1 Corinthians 7:26, 29-31). And he must have regarded his sufferings and theirs as the result of the Satanic-human hostility they encountered in the proclamation of the gospel (2 Corinthians 4:4; Ephesians 6:11-20; 1 Thessalonians 2:18; 2 Thessalonians 2:9-10). In a unique way and degree, because of his *divine office* (verse 25) and special commission as an apostle (see 1 Corinthians 9:17), he was supplying what was yet to be completed of the afflictions of the Messiah and his community in the time before the End.

Paul defines his special commission as being *a servant* and his message as *the word of God* concerning the *mystery hidden* for *ages and generations*. His task is to proclaim the content of this mystery everywhere. In pursuit of the task he toils mightily, utilizing the mighty strength that Christ supplies him (verse 29).

He describes the *mystery* as immensely great and rich (*the riches of the glory* [NRSV; NIV = *glorious riches*] *of this mystery*), says its content— formerly concealed—has now been made known by God to the *saints* (that is, God's holy people, believers in Christ)—not just to Paul himself—and defines the mystery as *Christ in you* [the Gentiles], *the hope of glory* (verse 27).

Both Gentiles and Jews talked much in Paul's day about mysteries: the former in cults with secret rites that were designed to communicate to initiates divine knowledge and life; and the latter about God's hidden purposes for the end time (Daniel 2:27-30, 47), which prophets and holy people (such as the "Right Teacher" of the community at Qumran by the Dead Sea) were commissioned by God to reveal. So Paul uses the term *mystery* in the sense of a revealed secret because it expresses the content of the Christian understanding of God's saving purpose in language that his contemporaries would understand (see also Romans 16:25-27; 1 Corinthians 2:6-10; Ephesians 1:9; 3:3-6).

Christ in you, the hope of glory, that is, Christ preached among the Gentiles or in a Gentile community's midst (2 Corinthians 1:19) is the basis of their hope of a glorious heavenly inheritance (Colossians 1:5, 12; 3:4).

But Paul so often spoke of the indwelling Christ (Romans 8:10; Ephesians 3:17) and the indwelling Spirit (Romans 8:9, 11; 1 Corinthians 6:19; 12:13) as a personal, as well as a community reality, that the personal dimension can scarcely be eliminated here. Both *among* and *in* the Gentiles are probably meant in this passage.

That the Gentiles were to be included in God's salvation was hardly a secret to Jews (Isaiah 2:2-4; 49:6; Zechariah 8:22-23). But what was unknown and was not being revealed by Paul and God's saints was the manner of the realization of this hope. The hope was that salvation would happen by the incorporation of Jews and Gentiles on the same basis—namely, faith in Jesus, the crucified/risen Messiah—and that in him they would form one unified body as the end-time people of God (see Ephesians 2:11-22).

Paul's Concern for the Colossians (2:1-5)

In 1:28 Paul speaks about his and others' (note the *we*) pastoral effort at bringing every Christian to full spiritual maturity in Christ. They proclaim, warn, and teach all (see also 1 Thessalonians 2:11-12).

The arduous character of their labors for the Colossians, the Laodiceans, and others personally unknown to Paul (2:1) is indicated by the words *labor* (NIV; NRSV = *toil*) and the twice-appearing *struggling*. The Greek word behind *toil* implies hard labor, and that behind *struggling* means to agonize, as in an athletic contest (1 Corinthians 9:25).

The goals of their strenuous endeavors are several: encouragement of heart, unity in love, deeper understanding of the divine mystery centering in Christ (for in him alone are the hidden treasures of divine wisdom and knowledge), and stability of faith in Christ in the face of the false teachers' convincing *arguments*.

§ § § § § § §

The Message of Colossians 1:24–2:5

Here we learn a great deal about Paul's understanding of Christian ministry. Some points refer to himself alone, some to his associates in ministry, and some to the church as a whole.

§ Paul is God-appointed, not self-appointed. He holds a divine office, given to him for the sake of others. His use of *we* (including Timothy) and his commendation of the faithful ministry in Christ of Epaphras (1:7; 4:12-13) and Tychicus (4:7) indicate that they, too, are God-commissioned as fellow-servants. However, their role as associates and representatives is different from his.

§ His task and theirs is to make the word of God fully known to every person under heaven.

§ This word concerns God's hitherto hidden, but now revealed, glorious purpose to save all people through Christ. When Christ comes to dwell in and among them, he becomes for them the hope of a heavenly inheritance.

§ God intends to save all people through Christ to his *saints* (the church), not simply to an elect person or group. Christians understand the revealed mystery and should grow in their understanding of it.

§ Suffering in the course of spreading the gospel in the world is part of the minister's calling. It is the consequence of hostility to the proclamation of the gospel, and it hastens the coming of the end time and the realization of the inheritance of the new age.

§ Christian ministers are to strive mightily in the power of Christ in proclaiming the gospel and bringing Christians to maturity of life in Christ. They are to protect God's people from false philosophies advanced in beguiling speech.

§ § § § § § §

Colossians 2:6-23

Introduction to These Verses

The Revised Standard Version assumes that verses 6-7 form the conclusion of verses 1-5 and that a new subject begins with verse 8. Many translations and commentators begin the new subject with 2:6. Actually, 2:6-7 is a transitional section. It summarizes what Paul has been saying in 1:24–2:5 and introduces what he is about to say in 2:8-15. Thus the text can be divided either way.

This section has three parts.
I. Transition (2:6-7)
II. Victory Over the Elemental Spirits (2:8-15)
III. Regulations of the Elemental Spirits (2:16-23)

Transition (2:6-7)

Verses 6-7 contain an appeal to Christian tradition. The Greek word behind *received* is a technical term that designates something handed down in an authoritative teaching and practice. In Judaism an equivalent Hebrew word was used to designate the handing down of the oral law (the rabbis' interpretation of the law of Moses) from one generation to another.

Christianity, as well as Judaism and Hellenism (2:8), had its traditions (see 1 Corinthians 11:2, 23; 2 Thessalonians 2:15; 3:6). Paul wants the Colossians to follow the Christian tradition (the apostolic gospel) about *Christ Jesus the Lord*, not *human tradition* (2:8). If they do, they will continue to live thankfully in Christ, be firmly rooted and established in him, and not be led astray by false teaching and practice.

Victory Over the Elemental Spirits (2:8-15)

Paul calls the false teachers' propaganda *philosophy* and *empty deceit (NRSV; NIV = hollow and deceptive philosophy)*.

The term *philosophy* was widely used in the Hellenistic world for almost any kind of religious thought and jargon claiming special knowledge of the universe and humankind's place in it. (The teachers at Colossae may have used the term to give status to their speculations.) In this broad usage the word did not signify serious critical thinking, like that of the great Greek philosophers of earlier times. Only the name was borrowed from them. Paul pillories this sort of human wisdom in 1 Corinthians 1:19-20.

Empty deceit characterizes the so-called *philosophy* as a hollow sham, without any content of truth and misleading to those who accept it. Paul viewed it as human, not divine, in origin.

This philosophy centered in *elemental spirits of the universe* (verse 8 NRSV; NIV = *basic principles of this world*). For Paul it stood in sharp antithesis to the divinely revealed truth about God's activity in Jesus Christ (*God's mystery*—1:26-27; 2:2).

Verse 9 repeats the affirmation of 1:19, but it adds the term *bodily* in order to suggest the manner in which the fullness dwells in Christ. Several interpretations of the meaning of this word here have been offered, the most plausible being: The whole fullness of deity dwells in Christ/church (the body); or *assuming bodily form* (becoming incarnate); or actually or genuinely, not in mere seeming. A reference to the historical incarnation hardly seems in view here, so the first and third, perhaps in combination, seem to approximate Paul's meaning.

Running like a thread through verses 9-15 is the phrase *in him* (or alternatively, *in whom* or *with him*). Throughout these verses Christ is made absolutely central and focal. God's fullness is in him. Believers experience fullness of life in him. Christ's circumcision (that is, death to the old life and resurrection to the new in baptism), forgiveness of sins, and escape from the indebtedness legally binding on us and from the bondage to the principalities and powers—all took place in him, with him, and through him. There is nothing that anyone could want from God that is not available in and through Christ. Why, then, would anyone look to elemental spirits? This is the general argument here.

Some phrases and concepts need explanation.

What is meant by the *the circumcision of Christ* and why is this concept introduced here (verse 11)? Were the heretics insisting on physical circumcision of Gentile believers in Christ, perhaps as a sacramental rite by which a person enters the Christian community and gains salvation? Does Paul mean to indicate that in his gospel—the true apostolic gospel—circumcision also has a place, but that it is circumcision of the heart, not of the body (Romans 2:28-29)? Probably.

Christian baptism is made here the counterpart to and replacement of Jewish circumcision. Unlike Jewish circumcision, it is *made without hands*; thus it is a divine work accomplished in the heart (on heart circumcision see Deuteronomy 10:16; Jeremiah 4:4; Ezekiel 44:7; Romans 2:28-29). In Jewish circumcision *the body of flesh*, that is, the old nature, the old sensual self, is put to death (Colossians 3:9; Romans 6:3-4; 7:24). In Christian baptism one dies with Christ and is raised to new life (Colossians 2:20; 3:1-3; Romans 6:6).

Paul's emphasis on the resurrection of believers as an accomplished fact (Colossians 1:13-14) is important. But the hope for the future is not exhausted by this fact.

There will also be a future resurrection and inheritance (1:5, 12; 2 Corinthians 4:14; Philippians 3:11).

What is meant by the legal change *against us* and God's *nailing it to the cross* (verse 14)?

The bond Paul refers to here is a certificate of indebtedness, an "IOU." It was issued in one's own handwriting by a debtor to a creditor, acknowledging a debt. References to such certificates appear in Hellenistic writings prior to Paul's time. Here in Colossians this certificate becomes a metaphor illustrating the sinner's relationship to God. Sinners have broken God's law and are in debt to God. They know through conscience that there is a legally binding IOU standing against them that they cannot pay. Paul the Pharisee himself groaned under his inability to meet God's requirements in the law (Romans 7:16, 22-23). A Jewish prayer contained the petition, "Our Father, our King, in your great mercy cancel all our debts."

Paul affirms here that this certificate of indebtedness has been cancelled (literally, *smeared out*, or *blotted out*), so that it can no longer accuse us. This was accomplished when God nailed it to the cross. The nailing to the cross may reflect the practice of affixing to the cross an inscription indicating the crime of the crucified one (Mark 15:26). The meaning is that because Jesus Christ was nailed to the cross for us, the debt has been canceled in and through his death (1 Corinthians 15:3; 2 Corinthians 5:21; Galatians 3:13).

Note that it is God who cancels the IOU. Salvation results from God's purposeful action, not from something people have done to appease an angry God.

In the cross God achieved not only the cancelling of the IOU but achieved victory over the principalities and powers. What happened to them, according to verse 15?

These powers are the same as the *elemental spirits of the universe* (2:8, 18, 20). They are viewed as hostile to Christ and God in that they demand placation and worship (verses 18, 20); and they possibly were believed by Paul to be in possession of the damning indictment (IOU). God *disarmed* (the Greek word literally means *stripped*) the principalities and powers of their authority and dignity and exposed their impotence for all to see and ridicule. God, in Christ, led them *like captives* in a victory procession. The Greek word behind *triumphing* suggests the triumphal procession of Roman conquerors through the streets of Rome to celebrate a military victory. In this victory march the vanquished were herded in humiliating exhibition after the victor's chariot (see 2 Corinthians 2:14).

However, the victory is one of subjection of the powers, not annihilation of them (2:10). This is yet to be accomplished at Christ's coming (1 Corinthians 15:24). Meanwhile Christians should know that the defeated powers have no ability to harm them. But they must constantly be on their guard lest they regain control over them (Ephesians 6:10-17).

Regulations of the Elemental Spirits (2:16-23)

If the powers that are believed to control the material world have been subjugated by Christ on the cross, then the practices associated with their worship have been done away with. Furthermore, by dying with Christ (verse 20), the Christian has escaped any authority these ruling spirits have. Death relieves one of all human controls (Romans 7:1-6; Galatians 2:19).

In addition, the regulations belong to an order that has been superseded. *These are only a shadow of what is to come; but the substance belongs to Christ* (verse 17). Paul (and other Christian teachers) adapted the Platonic idea that earthly shadows represent heavenly realities to his view of the succession of ages (this age and the age to come). Before Christ's coming the shadows pointed to the reality that was introduced with Christ's appearance (see Romans 5:14; Hebrews 10:1). Since Christ is the reality in the new age in which Christians now dwell (1:13), the foreshadowing has lost all right to exist and to exert authority. Therefore, Christians are free from ascetic regulations concerning food, drink, festivals, the worship of angels, and the arrogant revelations claimed by the heretical visionaries. Such prohibitions (taboos, verse 21) are of human origin and have no value in checking sensual indulgence.

§ § § § § § §

The Message of Colossians 2:6-23

The message can be summarized under three headings: what the Colossians were saved *from*; what they were saved *by*; and what they were saved *to*.

What they were saved from. They once lived in *the body of flesh* (verse 11 NRSV; NIV = *sinful nature*), that is, in a self or personality organized for and directed toward earthly things and hostile to God. They were *dead in trespasses* (acts violating God's commands) and, as Gentiles, were both inwardly and outwardly uncircumcised. Death is the state of the person outside Christ (Romans 6:13, 16, 20, 23). They were condemned by the certificate of indebtedness (the IOU of their conscience over their violation of the will of God), which they could not pay off. They were under bondage to cosmic powers and the ascetic rules and regulations associated with their worship (verse 20).

What they were saved by. The savior is *Christ Jesus the Lord* (verse 6), who is the complete embodiment of *deity* (verse 9). In baptism they died with Christ and *through faith in the power of God* they were raised with Christ (verse 12). All of this was God's doing through the cross of Christ. Through that cross God in Christ broke the hold of the principalities and powers over the life of the Colossians and by his free forgiveness cancelled the IOU.

Human beings are not saved by human wisdom and tradition (verses 8, 22) concerning the cosmic powers or through visions, regulations, and practices their devotees proffer. They are saved only by holding fast to the head (of the church and all cosmic powers—1:18; 2:10).

What they were saved to. The result of their baptismal faith-union with Christ is variously put: *fulness* of life (verse 9), that is, participation in the same fullness of life (powers, graces) that was in Christ himself; circumcision of the heart (verse 11), that is, humble response to God and the total obedience to God's will that produces inner goodness, not simply outward correctness; freedom from the old sensual nature (verses 11, 23), from guilt before God due to acts of disobedience to God's revealed will (verse 14), and from cramping, ineffective, ascetic, human regulations (verses 16-23); and, above all, union with the one who is the source and nourisher of church/cosmic life and unity (verse 19).

§ § § § § § §

Colossians 3:1-17

Introduction to These Verses

Up to this point in the letter the supremacy and all-sufficiency of Christ have been asserted as a counter to the claim of the false teachers that other potencies must be recognized and honored by Christians. The writer has made it clear that *Christ is all, and in all* (3:11).

How then will this belief affect the Christians' everyday life in this world? The answer is given in 3:1–4:6. Some of this answer will be considered in Part Eleven and the rest in Part Twelve.

These verses may be divided into three parts.
  I. The New Life in Christ (3:1-4)
 II. Putting Off the Old Nature (3:5-11)
III. Putting On the New Nature (3:12-17)

The New Life in Christ (3:1-4)

This paragraph summarizes and highlights affirmations made before: that Christians have died with Christ (2:12, 20) and have been raised with him (2:12). It points out where the Christians' attention and emphasis should be in the light of their union with Christ and their membership in *the kingdom of his* [God's] *beloved Son* (1:13).

The *if* of 3:1, in the Greek text, suggests no element of doubt about the reality of the death/resurrection of believers through union with their Lord.

The verbs *seek* and *set your minds* are expressed here in the Greek tense that suggests continuous effort.

The two realms of life and activity on which people set their minds, according to this passage, are the heavenly and the earthly worlds.

Life in the heavenly world, says Paul, centers in the resurrected and exalted Christ and concerns itself with what is pleasing to him, God's honored Messiah (verse 1). The heavenly world was thought in Paul's time to be the realm of all that is ultimately essential and real, transcendent, and associated with God.

The earth was believed to be the shadow of the heavenly reality (in Hellenism) or the arena in which sin and death are active (in Judaism, based in part on Genesis 3:17-19; 6:1-8; and the growing mythology in intertestamental literature about fallen angels and the rapacious demons that issued from them to plague the earth). The contrast between the two worlds is especially evident in the Gospel of John and the First Letter of John (John 8:23; 12:25; 1 John 2:15-17; 5:19).

For Paul the material world (matter) is not essentially evil, as the Colossian heretics apparently believed, but it is the place where demons and other powers operate in seducing people into false worship and leading them into evil attitudes and acts (2 Corinthians 4:4; Galatians 4:8-9; Ephesians 6:10-17). Here both the earthly and the heavenly are characterized in ethical terms: as what is un-Godlike and un-Christlike in spirit and activity, on the one hand, and Godlike and Christlike, on the other (3:5-17).

Since Christians are citizens of heaven, now living for a while on earth (Philippians 3:20-21) and awaiting their heavenly inheritance (Colossians 1:5, 12; 3:4), they should keep a steady eye on their destiny. They should live by the standards of that order to which they already belong, and await the full realization and manifestation of what they will be after the coming of Christ (3:4).

Putting Off the Old Nature (3:5-11)

What the Christian life is *not* like is set forth first.

The Colossians are exhorted to *put to death* (verse 5), to *get rid of* (verse 8), and *to take off* (verse 9) the *old nature* with its attitudes and practices. In baptism they died and rose with Christ (2:12). As his life thereafter was totally new, so must theirs be. In baptism they laid aside, as an old garment, the old self and its attitudes and practices. They were clothed with the new garment of righteousness and life. They must realize this and live and act accordingly (Romans 6:11).

The *old nature* (verse 9), or the *old self,* according to Paul, is rebellious against God, worships the creature rather than the Creator, is sin- and Satan-dominated, follows selfish desires, and is incorporated in the old, corrupt, earthbound humanity descended from Adam (Romans 1:18-32; 1 Corinthians 15:45-50).

The earthly (or earthward) attitudes and practices are listed here twice in groups of five each (verses 5, 8). There is also a fivefold enumeration of virtues or graces (verse 12). Paul may be following here a traditional pattern, perhaps derived ultimately from old Iranian religion, in which a person's good and bad deeds are listed in fives. He does not mean the lists to be exhaustive, but only suggestive of the nature of earthly and heavenly living.

In listing the earthly vices (verse 5) Paul moves from outward acts to inward attitudes, as Jesus did in the Sermon on the Mount (Matthew 5:21-48). The basic inner sin listed here is covetousness, which is called *idolatry.* Covetousness is idolatry in that it involves the setting of one's affections on earthly things, rather than on God and Christ. It puts some created object of desire, possessed by someone else, in the place that God/Christ alone should occupy.

The second list (verse 8) has to do with social attitudes—attitudes that destroy loving social relationships. Abusive, foul, and deceptive language is especially noted as characteristic of the old nature. Jesus and the early church put a high premium on simple, truthful, edifying speech (Matthew 5:33-37; Ephesians 4:29; Colossians 4:6; James 5:12). Words are the self in extension; by them others can experience for good or ill what we are really like inside.

Putting On the New Nature (3:12-17)

At the end of the preceding paragraph (verse 10) the new nature or self is said to be constantly *renewed in . . . the image of its creator.* There is clearly an allusion here to Genesis 1:26-27, where Adam is said to have been created in the image of God.

Both the Old and the New Testaments indicate that it is God's purpose that humankind should be like God. But this was not realized through the first Adam (Romans 5:12-14). Paul declares that it was accomplished through the second Adam, Jesus Christ (Romans 5:18-19; 1 Corinthians 15:22), who is himself the image of God (2 Corinthians 4:4; Colossians 1:15). Christ transforms those who believe in him into his own image (Romans 8:29; 1 Corinthians 15:49; 2 Corinthians 3:18). This transformation, which was begun in the baptismal death/resurrection with Christ (Colossians 2:11-12), goes forward daily in the sufferings and tribulations of Christian life and service: *inwardly we are being renewed day by day* (2 Corinthians 4:16). The Christian possesses God-likeness and also goes on to it (Ephesians 5:1; Philippians 3:12; Colossians 3:10).

A result of putting on the new nature and of the growing likeness to God and Christ is increasing *knowledge* (verse 10). That is, we see *the mystery hidden for ages and generations* concerning Christ as God's agent in the salvation of the Gentiles (1:26-27; 2:2-3). We know how to *lead a life worthy of the Lord, fully pleasing to him, bearing fruit in every good work* (1:10). Knowledge of this sort was radically different from that offered by the false teachers.

This God-likeness and knowledge of God's will for life is available to all members of the new humanity— whatever their racial, religious, cultural, and social background and status—through Christ who is absolutely everything and permeates everything (3:11).

As the chosen, holy, and beloved people of God the Colossians are to clothe themselves five virtues or graces (3:12). Through these the new nature manifests itself. These virtues are similar to Paul's fruits of the Spirit, mentioned in Galatians 5:22-23. They are attitudes and actions elsewhere attributed to God and Christ (Romans 2:4; 2 Corinthians 10:1; Philippians 2:8). Thus the imitation of God and Christ is enjoined again.

To the five attributes Paul adds others: forbearance and forgiveness; love (*above all*); peace; thankfulness; and sharing in instruction, admonition, worship, and Christian activity.

§ § § § § § §

The Message of Colossians 3:1-17

The thought of Paul's letters oscillates among four centers. Briefly put, they are: You were; you are; you must; you will be. It is easy to identify these four centers in 3:1-17 and elsewhere in the letter.

(1) *You were.* You once had your minds set on earthly things: fornication, impurity, passions, evil desire, and covetousness; in these you once walked, when you lived in them (3:7). Your old nature expressed itself in anger, wrath, malice, slander, foul talk, lying, and social divisiveness (3:8-11).

Earlier he had told them that they were living in the dominion of darkness (1:13), separated from God and God's people and hostile in mind, doing evil deeds (1:21), uncircumcised in heart and dead in sin (2:11-13), guilty before God's law (2:14), and under bondage to the elemental spirits (2:20).

The picture of their former life is similar to that painted in the letter to the Ephesians, chapter 2, where the readers are said to have been without hope and *without God in the world* (Ephesians 2:12).

(2) *You are.* Whereas you were once dead, you are now alive (2:10, 13) through resurrection with Christ (3:1). You are participating in his resurrection life as a present reality. You are united to the glorified and exalted Christ and are seated with him, though in a hidden way, in God's very presence in heaven (3:1, 3). Your earthly life is also a heavenly life—right now! (See also Ephesians 2:6.)

You have a new nature, which is growing into the likeness of God and coming to full knowledge of God's will (3:10). You are fully forgiven (2:13; 3:13), God's holy and beloved chosen people (3:12), members of a community without racial, religious, and social distinctions (3:11), released from the ascetic regulations imposed by the elemental spirits of the universe (2:20-23), and heirs of a glorious future *stored up for you in heaven* (1:5, 12).

This all came about through your faith in God and your baptismal identification with Christ in his death on the cross and his resurrection by the power of God (2:11-15).

Salvation for Paul was not just a "someday" experience, but to a large degree a present one.

(3) *You must.* Paul's *therefore* (2:16; 3:5, 12) links present reality to present obligation. If you are God's transformed chosen ones, you have an obligation to live in a way pleasing to God and to Christ, (1:10; 3:17), to bear the fruit of good works (1:10), to have and exercise the graces that belong to members of Christ's kingdom (1:13; 3:12-17), to grow in knowledge of the truth (1:9-10; 2:2-3; 3:10), and to promote unity in Christ's body, the church (3:11, 14-15).

Maturity in Christ for every person was Paul's driving passion (1:28-29).

(4) *You will be.* While salvation for Paul was a present reality, it was also for him a future goal. In its final fullness it will be given by Christ at his coming (3:4). Life in the final Kingdom is the *inheritance of the saints in light* (1:12). Christians and all people will be judged by God and Christ (1:22, 28; 3:6; see Romans 14:10-12; 2 Corinthians 5:10). Their maturity (perfection) in Christ will be supremely important on that day (1:22, 28). Both Paul and the Colossian Christians have the responsibility to promote maturity in the church (1:28-29; 3:12-17, especially verse 16).

The nature of the final salvation is expressed in a few great terms: *inheritance* (promised to God's people in the Old Testament), *light* (the light of God's presence—1:12), *glory* (splendor, radiance from God's presence—1:27; 3:4), and *fulness* of life (2:10).

§ § § § § § §

PART TWELVE   Colossians 3:18–4:18

Introduction to These Chapters

Though Paul exhorted the Colossian Christians to concentrate attention on heavenly things, rather than earthly ones (3:1-4), he did not understand Christianity as a way of fleeing from this world, as countless religious mystics and ascetics have tried to do.

For him Christianity was rather a way of redeeming the world, according to the intention of its Creator and Redeemer (Romans 8:19-22; 12:2; Ephesians 2). He rejoiced that Christian communities were being planted throughout the Roman Empire (Colossians 1:5-6) and that they were shining as lights in the world (Philippians 2:15). He recognized the responsibility of Christians to support the God-ordained political authorities and to live as responsible citizens, even to the paying of taxes and other obligations (Romans 13:1-8*a*). Proper relations with the neighbor were important to him (Romans 13:8*b*-10). Likewise important were relationships within Christian households and among Christian workers and churches.

This section of Colossians has four main parts.
  I. Rules for the Christian Household (3:18–4:1)
 II. Counsels on Prayer and Witnessing (4:2-6)
III. Greetings from Paul and Associates (4:7-17)
 IV. Authentication and Benediction (4:18)

Paul's point of view seems to be: Though human life in this world may not continue long (Romans 13:11-14; 1 Corinthians 7:29-31), it is to be lived in all of its dimensions as long as it lasts. It is to be lived according to the pattern ordained by its Creator—a pattern revealed in the Holy Scriptures, in Jesus Christ, in the church's apostolic tradition, in his own inspired experience, and in the best insights of contemporary culture.

Rules for the Christian Household (3:18–4:1)

This short section contains the earliest Christian prescriptions for family life known to us. Others are contained in Ephesians 5:22–6:9 (perhaps an elaboration of Colossians 3:18–4:1); 1 Timothy 2:8-15; 6:1-2; Titus 2:1-10; 1 Peter 2:18–3:7); and in writings of early (second century) Christian fathers.

Paul and other early Christian teachers seem to have appropriated and assimilated to the Christian point of view some of the best ethical standards of their time. Hellenistic writers (particularly the Stoics) often enumerated duties that conscientious people should fulfill in order to live in harmony with one another and with the universe. In synagogues of the Hellenistic world, Jewish teachers spelled out God's requirements for family and social life in terms and concepts partly borrowed from popular Hellenistic ethics. And early Christians acknowledged those standards of life that were widely adjudged to be reasonable and right.

While the content of Hellenistic-Jewish ethics and of Christian ethics have much in common, the latter has a unique perspective.

First, the motivation is different. Christians who are *in the Lord* (verse 18) are to do what pleases the Lord (verse 20). They are to fear the Lord (verse 22) and serve the Lord (verses 22-24). From the Lord they will receive the inheritance as a *reward* (verse 24). Since *Christ is all, and in all* (3:11), their lives are lived in his presence and they will give an account to him. They are to do the things that are pleasing to him (1:10).

Second, the superiors have obligations to the inferiors,

not simply the other way around. There are rights and duties on both sides. The rights of wives, children, and slaves are as real as those of husbands, fathers, and masters.

Third, though love is mentioned only once in the household rules here (verse 19), Paul evidently understood love to be the central ingredient in harmonious and effective domestic life (verse 14). Love, for Paul, is that unselfish, other-regarding attitude that puts others' interests ahead of one's own—the kind of attitude Christ had (Philippians 2:3-11).

Three sets of relationships are treated here: wives and husbands, children and fathers, and slaves and masters.

The directive here to wives and husbands leaves no doubt that Paul accepted the Old Testament perspective of the husband's leadership in the family. This is plain from 1 Corinthians 11:2-12, where he appeals to Genesis 2:18 and 2:21-23. He evidently believed that equality before God in redemption (Galatians 3:28) does not eliminate distinctions inherent in Creation and that women should accept the position divinely assigned to them.

In actual practice Paul gave women a high place in his thought and activity (Acts 16:11-15; Romans 16; Galatians 3:28; Philippians 4:2-3), as did Jesus. The statements in 1 Corinthians 14:34-35 are directed against chatter and irrelevant questions in the worship service, not against the right of women to participate (to prophesy and pray) publicly. That right was admitted by Paul in 1 Corinthians 11:2-16.

Paul did not seek basic changes in the social order of his time—the world was hardly prepared for either the feminist or the abolitionist (antislavery) movements—but he sowed seeds of equality that eventually bore fruit in both. (See his letter to Philemon.) Here, his direction to husbands to love and be considerate of their wives—in the sense in which he understood love and kindness—introduced a new and transformative element into marriage. (See also Ephesians 5:21-23.)

The injunctions to slaves and masters occupies a large place in this section of household rules, probably because of the large numbers of slaves in society and in Christian congregations of the time. It has been estimated that there were 200,000 to 300,000 slaves in Rome by Paul's day, amounting to about one-third of the total population. There were major slave insurrections in the second and first centuries B.C.

Paul affirms that both masters and slaves stand under the authority of the Lord. Slaves must render faithful service, for they are really serving the Lord; and masters must be just and fair in their treatment of the slaves. Masters, too, have a Master in heaven and will be judged by the same standards as slaves (3:25). In his letter to Philemon Paul elevates the converted slave Onesimus to a place of equality with himself (Philemon 17). He appeals for Philemon's acceptance of him as *a beloved brother* (Philemon 16).

Counsel on Prayer and Witnessing (4:2-6)

Watchfulness and thanksgiving appear here as essential elements in persevering prayer. Being watchful means being vigilant, as opposed to being lethargic or sleepy. It may have the additional meaning of being alert for the coming of the Lord, as in 1 Thessalonians 5:6.

For Paul thanksgiving was always a dominant element in prayer (Colossians 1:3; 3:17; Romans 1:8-9; Philippians 1:3-5).

Here, as elsewhere in his letters (Romans 15:30-31, for example), he asks his readers for their prayer support of him in his ministry of declaring *the mystery of Christ,* that is, the revealed secret of God's activity in Jesus Christ for the redemption of the whole world. He seems to hope still for deliverance from prison and a continued ministry.

The Colossians also are to have a part in the spreading

of the gospel. They must behave *wisely* (that is, in full conformity with God's will—1:9-10; 2:2-3; 3:16) toward non-Christians (giving a testimony by the quality of their life). And they must speak graciously and effectively to those who inquire concerning their faith and life (see 1 Peter 3:15).

Making the most of (4:5) is literally *buying up* or *snapping up*—a term from the marketplace. *The time* is the present opportunity, which may not last long (1 Corinthians 7:29). The spread of the gospel was an urgent matter in the period before the End (see 2 Thessalonians 2:2).

Greetings From Paul and Associates (4:7-17)

Paul was not alone in his prison experience. Aristarchus (verse 10) and Epaphras (Philemon 23), at least, were incarcerated also. The many other associates mentioned here were free to visit Paul, offer him comfort (verse 11), and accept assignments of various sorts from him. Several persons are worthy of brief comment.

Aristarchus, (John) Mark, and Jesus (Justus) were Jewish Christians who had remained loyal to Paul (apparently when other Jewish Christians had renounced him because of his abandonment of law observance as a requisite for Christian salvation). For information about Aristarchus see Acts 19:29; 20:4; 27:2; Philemon 24; and for John Mark see Acts 12:12, 25; 15:37-39; 2 Timothy 4:11; Philemon 24; 1 Peter 5:13. Nothing is known about Jesus (Justus) outside this passage. The three are said by Paul to have been special sources of comfort to him. We may guess that they valiantly supported his position and may have been especially attentive to him.

Three Gentile Christians are mentioned next: Epaphras, Luke, and Demas. Epaphras, the founder of the Colossian church, undoubtedly was under attack by the Colossian false teachers. Paul here strongly supports his work as a true servant of Christ at Colossae, Laodicea, and Hierapolis. He mentions his (Epaphras's) continuing concern for those churches. Luke (see also Philemon 24; 2 Timothy 4:11), only here in the New Testament referred to as a physician, is the traditional author of the two-volume work Luke–Acts. Demas (see also Philemon 24) is said in 2 Timothy 4:10 to have deserted Paul for worldly reasons.

Tychicus (4:7; see also Acts 20:4; Ephesians 6:21; 2 Timothy 4:12; Titus 3:12), Paul's special emissary to the Colossian church and probable bearer of this letter, is being sent as a source of information about Paul and of direction and encouragement in the present church crisis. He is also evidently to front for the returning runaway slave, Onesimus, and to deliver to Philemon a letter about him.

Nothing is known about Nympha and the church in her house (verse 15).

Archippus (verse 17; see also Philemon 2) may have been acting head of the churches of the Lycus valley during the absence of Epaphras. Paul urges him here to a faithful discharge of his calling.

The letter to Laodicea (verse 16) has been thought by some to be our Ephesians or our Philemon; but it probably has not been preserved.

Authentication and Benediction (4:18)

As was customary at the time, letter writers who used a scribe added a conclusion in the writer's own hand (see also 1 Corinthians 16:21; Galatians 6:11; 2 Thessalonians 3:17; Philemon 19). For Paul it served to drive home points (*remember my chains*), to certify the origin of the letter in the face of possible forgeries (2 Thessalonians 2:2), and to conclude letters with a personal touch.

§ § § § § § §

The Message of Colossians 3:18–4:18

§ Christianity is not just a way of thinking about God and human existence; it is also a way of living in this world. What we do in our time on earth is important to God and determines our destiny.

§ Earthly life is to be lived according to the pattern ordained by its Creator; knowledge of God's will is given to those who seek it.

§ The kind of life that is appropriate for this world is Christlike life. We are to live in a manner pleasing to him. This way of living is not inevitably in conflict with all prevailing social values, but often affirms and reinforces some of them.

§ People of every class and condition are accountable to God/Christ for the way they act toward one another.

§ The rights of weak and oppressed people are as important as those of the strong and the privileged.

§ Love and just treatment of others are the central ingredients of harmonious and effective domestic life.

§ All legitimate work, whatever one's station in life, should be done conscientiously as a service to the Lord Christ, not just to please human masters or employers.

§ Persevering and thankful prayer can promote individual and church stability and growth, and can assist fellow Christians in their work of spreading the gospel.

§ Careful Christian living and gracious witnessing are the keys to effective evangelizing of the outside world.

§ The fellowship of Christian life and service is rich beyond measure. It knows no boundaries of race, class, or gender. It strengthens and encourages the participants, and leads to Christian maturity and full assurance in all the will of God (4:12).

§ § § § § § §

Introduction to 1 Thessalonians

The Church at Thessalonica

Thessalonica, modern Thessaloniki, located at the head of the Thermaic Gulf of the Aegean Sea in Macedonia, was founded about 316 B.C. by Cassander, a general in Alexander the Great's army. He named the city after his wife, the daughter of Philip II and half-sister of Alexander.

In 146 B.C., when Macedonia became a Roman province, the city became the capital of the new province. Its location on the Via Egnatia, the famous East-West road, plus its harbor facilities, made it a prosperous trade and political center.

Many religions (advocating the worship of Greek, Roman, and oriental gods, and even Yahweh of the Jews) vied for acceptance and loyalty by the cosmopolitan populace. The Jewish population there was a considerable one. In the Roman period a civic cult praised Roman rulers (especially Julius Caesar and Augustus) and prominent patrons of Rome and exalted the goddess Roma.

The location of the synagogue where Paul preached is unknown. It may have been near an agora (marketplace) close to the harbor area.

Paul, Silvanus (Silas), and Timothy came into this politically and religiously charged atmosphere on Paul's second missionary journey (Acts 17:1-9), after a disastrous experience in Philippi (Acts 16:11-40; 1 Thessalonians 2:2). Paul preached in the synagogue for three sabbaths and evidently remained in the city for some time thereafter. He was there long enough to have worked intensively at his trade (1 Thessalonians 2:9) and to have received financial help more than once from the Philippians (Philippians 4:16). We may guess that he and his companions were there for two or three months.

Paul argued in the synagogue that the Old Testament predicts the coming of a suffering messiah and that Jesus of Nazareth fulfilled this expectation (Acts 17:3). Some Jews and also many god-fearing Gentiles were convinced, as well as a number of influential women. The Gentiles, male and female, were attracted to Judaism by its worship of one God (monotheism) and its high religious and ethical teaching. However, they did not accept the full yoke of the Jewish law (circumcision, sabbath observance, and the food laws). They were excellent prospects for Paul's law-free gospel about Jesus.

Paul's proclamation about the present and coming rule of Jesus Christ provoked unbelieving and jealous Jews to twist a religious affirmation into a political charge of disloyalty to Caesar and into mob action directed against Paul, his companions, and their host Jason. When Paul and his associates could not be found, Jason and other Christians were brought before the city authorities and forced to put up money to guarantee the good conduct of their guests. For the good of all Paul and his companions immediately left the city by night. The infant church was thus put in a precarious position almost from birth.

When Paul arrived at Athens, after a mission in Beroea (Acts 17:10-15), he sent Timothy back to Thessalonica to assist the infant congregation and to bring him word of its condition (1 Thessalonians 3:1-5). Paul then crossed over to Corinth and began preaching there. Later Timothy brought a letter to him from the Thessalonians, inquiring about some important matters, to which Paul responded in 1 Thessalonians, chapters 4–5.

First Thessalonians is Paul's joyful reaction to the news of the fidelity of the Thessalonians in spite of their sufferings. It is also Paul's attempt to guide the Thessalonians to a fuller Christian life through a solution to their problems. It is a pastoral letter.

The Problems in the Church at Thessalonica

(1) Persecution by fellow townsmen, probably spearheaded by the unbelieving Jews who had forced Paul from the city (Acts 17:5; 1 Thessalonians 2:14-16; 3:3-4).

(2) Doubts about the integrity of the missionaries, spread probably by the hostile Jews (1 Thessalonians 2).

(3) Confusion about the validity of their new faith and experience in the light of Jewish attacks (1 Thessalonians 1:4-10); about the Christian view of the future (the fate of Christians who have died before the coming of Christ, the time of Christ's coming, and Christian activity meanwhile—4:13–5:11); and about the place of suffering in the life of Christians (3:3-4).

(4) Sexual irregularities (4:3-8), idleness and troublemaking (4:11-12), carelessness (5:1-11), and quarreling (5:13).

Date and Place of Writing

This letter is probably the earliest of the preserved letters of Paul, though this honor has been claimed (without adequate proof) for the letter to the Galatians. First Thessalonians dates to A.D. 50 or 51, and was written by Paul from Corinth.

1 Thessalonians 1

Introduction to These Verses

The letter begins in the usual Pauline fashion. The writers are Paul, Silvanus (Silas), and Timothy, all three of whom were present at the founding of the church there (Acts 16:1-5; 17:1-15).

Silvanus is the Latinized form of the Greek-Semitic name *Silas*. In Acts, Luke uses the latter form of the name, by which he was known in Jerusalem, but Paul uses the form appropriate to the Gentile world of the time. Silvanus was a Roman citizen, like Paul (Acts 16:37-38), a Jew by birth, and an important leader (prophet) in the Jerusalem church (Acts 15:22-35). He functioned at times either as a scribe or a trusted secretary or both (1 Peter 5:12). He may have played some part in the actual writing of First Thessalonians.

The statement that the Thessalonian church is *in God the Father and the Lord Jesus Christ* (verse 1) means that it is in vital union with them both. That it is *in God* would refute the allegations of the hostile Jews that the church is really of human, not divine, origin. That it is *in the Lord Jesus Christ* would affirm against them that Jesus of Nazareth is in truth the messiah predicted in the Holy Scriptures. Even the greeting of the letter is designed to be reassuring to the Thessalonians.

The thanksgiving for the Thessalonians, which begins with verse 2, runs intermittently all the way to 3:10. However, it is not pure thanksgiving. Intertwined with it is argument, meant to convince the readers that their conversion and Christian status are a genuine work of God, not of insincere, mercenary charlatans who have misled and exploited them. This apologetic (defensive) note appears first in verse 5b. It becomes dominant in chapters 2 and 3, with touches of thanksgiving in 2:13 and 3:9 and in a few other places.

The description of the Thessalonians' conversion experience serves this apologetic purpose. The central idea of verses 2-10 may be put as follows: We give thanks for the conclusive evidence that you Thessalonians have a secure place in God's great redemptive plan. This evidence consists of the striking nature of your conversion experience and the character of its fruits.

The conversion experience is described at some length.

First, the gospel was preached to them both in word and by life. It came to them not simply in human language but in words directed and empowered by the Holy Spirit through men who were imitators of the Lord and God-possessed (verses 5-6). It was not "just talk," such as a huckster of ideas might deliver (2 Corinthians 2:17; 4:2). Therefore, it was the kind of message that was potent enough to evoke faith and transform life.

Second, the Thessalonians' response to this powerful preaching of the gospel is described. They, like the proclaimers, were fully convinced of its truth and power (the message came *with full conviction*). They then began to copy the missionaries and the Lord.

Paul believed that his gospel led to personal transformation according to a basic pattern revealed in successive manifestations: first in God (Ephesians 5:1; Colossians 3:10); then in Jesus Christ, who is the image (likeness) of God (2 Corinthians 4:4-6; Colossians 1:15); and then in believers, God's children (Romans 8:29; 1 Corinthians 15:49). For Paul, Christians are not those who have just a new set of ideas about God and the world and certain novel and thrilling emotional experiences (though they may have these). The Christian is one who *in character* has become like other Christians, who are like Christ, who is like God. God/Christlikeness is the ultimate goal (Ephesians 5:1-2).

Paul, Timothy, and Silvanus, then, were not insufferable egotists when they asked people to imitate them (verse 6 here; see also 1 Corinthians 4:16; 11:1; Philippians 3:17; 4:9). If Christianity is a way of becoming and being like Christ and God, all Christians are examples to be imitated, whether they want to be or not. So the Thessalonians immediately *became an example* to others (verse 7).

Third, the fruits of their remarkable conversion are presented. There is joy, inspired by the Holy Spirit, in the midst of affliction. For both Jesus and Paul, joy in suffering is an essential mark of a Christian (Matthew 5:11-12; Romans 5:3), inescapable evidence that by God's strength one has mastered fear and untoward circumstances.

There are *faith*, *love*, and *hope* (verse 3; see also 5:8), the most important of Christian qualities (1 Corinthians 13:13). Each manifests itself in practical ways.

By their welcome of the missionaries, their abandonment of idols, and their new service of the true God they have become an example for the believers in Macedonia, Achaia (the Roman province, consisting of the lower half of Greece), and everywhere (verse 8). Their conversion has borne witness to the reality of new life in Christ, has given weight to the Christian hope of final salvation (verse 10), and has offered irrefutable proof of their divine election (God's initiative in reaching out to save those who will hear and respond). They have become a part of the people of God, by God's intention.

The reference to the coming of Christ appears like a refrain in the letter (1:10; 2:19; 3:13; 5:23) and broadens into a considerable discussion near its end (4:13–5:11). That Paul and his associates talked much about this subject when they were in Thessalonica is evident from his own words (2 Thessalonians 2:5) and from the crisis with which he had to deal in 2 Thessalonians. Paul seems to have believed that the church is the outpost of the coming kingdom of God.

§ § § § § § §

The Message of 1 Thessalonians 1

This passage must have been highly enlightening and reassuring to the Thessalonians, and it may be so to us. Noteworthy are the following emphases.

§ The deep concern of Paul for his beloved children (see 2:11), his constant prayers and his thanksgiving for them, and his unabashed praise of their spiritual state and their witness in the world. The Christian fellowship (note the frequent term *brothers*) was obviously very dear to him (2:17; 3:7-9) and ought to be to us.

§ The blessed assurance that Christians have, that God loves them and had ordained that they should have a place in God's great redemptive plan (verse 4).

§ The clear definition of the true nature and results of Christian conversion, which here are presented as the receiving of the word of God through the preaching of Spirit-empowered messengers, deep inner joy inspired by the Holy Spirit, the presence in the Christian of the fruits of the Spirit (faith, love, and hope) and the practical results in daily life to which they lead, the radical change in one's outward manner of life, and the influence of converts on others.

§ The strange and wonderful presence in the heart of joy in the midst of affliction.

§ The glorious hope for the future, centering in the resurrected Lord, which should be cherished and kept alive by Christians.

§ § § § § § §

1 Thessalonians 2:1-16

Introduction to These Verses

Paul's thanksgiving for the Thessalonians was almost completely thrown off track by the section of the letter we now encounter. As he dictated the letter, his joy over the Thessalonians' deep inner transformation (1:5-6) and the striking change in their outward manner of life (1:7-10) became stifled by thoughts about what had happened to the church after his departure.

Grievous troubles for the church had set in. Their fellow countrymen had begun to persecute them (2:14; 3:3-4). Paul's outburst against the Jews (2:14-16) implies that they were instigating the persecution and working through Thessalonian Gentiles to achieve their ends.

What exactly this persecution consisted of we do not know. Were the Jews continuing to press charges, probably of disloyalty to Caesar and Rome (Acts 17:7), before the *politarchs* (the Greek word for *city officials* in Acts 17:6, 8)? In the territory of Macedonia the politarchs were the local, non-Roman magistrates of a free city, who would be anxious to maintain the favor of their Roman benefactors by suppressing any indication of disloyalty to Rome.

More certain is the indication from Paul's remarks here that hostile Jews were spreading lies about Paul and his companions—about their motives, conduct, and the truth of their gospel.

Thus Paul moves quickly in the letter to present

evidence that he and his associates are true servants of God. They are entirely above reproach in the conduct of their ministry at Thessalonica and in their attitudes toward and dealings with the Thessalonians after they left there.

This section of the letter has two parts.
I. The Ministry at Thessalonica (2:1-12)
II. Imitators of the Judean Churches (2:13-16)

The Ministry at Thessalonica (2:1-12)

Here Paul bares his soul to the Thessalonians. We see not only how he understood Christian ministry in general, but also how he and his colleagues performed in the light of this understanding.

(1) *It was a courageous, God-ordained ministry.* Paul suggests that the shameful beating and imprisonment at Philippi (Acts 16:19-40)—the personal indignity accorded him and Silas as Roman citizens—and the *strong opposition* encountered at Thessalonica (Acts 17:1-9) would surely have intimidated and silenced self-appointed and self- serving persons. But this kind of treatment would not have affected the work of messengers whom God had truly appointed to this work (verse 2). And the results show, he says, that God was active in our ministry among you (verse 1).

(2) *It was a sound and faithful ministry.* Their *appeal* (persuasive preaching) did not *spring from error,* (NIV; NRSV = *deceit*) probably meaning here from erroneous interpretation of the Scriptures. Paul had taught that Jesus of Nazareth fulfilled prophetic hopes concerning the coming of the messiah (Acts 17:3), a view many Jews violently opposed. For them an unlettered, crucified felon could not possibly be their glorious, triumphant coming King (John 7:15; 1 Corinthians 1:23).

The denial that their preaching sprang from *impure motives* implies that some sort of sexual accusations had been made against the missionaries. Paul's doctrine of Christian freedom from the law, the widespread moral looseness at all levels of society in Hellenistic life, the practice of religious prostitution in temples of the Gentile world, and a degree of openness—foreign to Judaism—in relationships between the sexes in Christian churches may have led to charges of this sort.

No trickery (deceit, cunning, trickery) or *flattery*, commonly employed by traveling hucksters of philosophy and religion (Acts 13:6-12; 16:16-18; 2 Corinthians 2:17; 4:2; 11:20), marred the sincerity of their proclamation. The missionaries' aim was to please God, their judge, not to please people (verse 4).

(3) *It was a selfless and self-giving ministry.* Their words were never *a ruse for greed* (verse 5), that is, a way of camouflaging greed. God was their witness! They did not use their rights as *apostles of Christ* to obtain honor and financial support (see 1 Corinthians 9:3-18; 2 Corinthians 11:7-11). Rather, out of love for them, like a nursing mother taking care of her children, they shared not only the gospel but their very selves as well.

(4) *It was a self-supporting ministry.* Paul worked long hours at his trade (tentmaking, according to Acts 18:3, though some scholars think it was leather-working). Whether Silas and Timothy worked with him or at something else is not said. Their objective was to be financially independent of the Thessalonians. Paul knew that, as an apostle of Christ, he had a right to live off the gospel (1 Corinthians 9:3-14). But he staunchly refused to do so in order that he might not put hinder *the gospel of Christ* (1 Corinthians 9:12). People might think he was in it for the money.

(5) *It was an educative ministry, through personal example and patient exhortation and encouragement.* In their personal lives they were role models (holy, righteous, blameless) and, like a father with children (exhorting, encouraging, charging), they sought patiently to bring them to mature

Christian living—to a life pleasing to God and befitting their membership in God's kingdom.

Imitators of the Judean Churches (2:13-16)

In two respects the Thessalonian Christians imitated the Judean churches: in their wholehearted response to the active and effective word of God (verse 13), and in their patient acceptance of suffering at the hands of unbelieving Jews (verse 14).

The Christian churches of Judea mentioned here, in Paul's mind, must have included the Jerusalem church (Galatians 1:18-24). Paul knew of the suffering there at the time of the martyrdom of Stephen; indeed, according to the Book of Acts (7:58–8:3; 9:1-2), he himself had a major role in it. There was also persecution under Herod Agrippa I in A.D. 41–44 (Acts 12:1-5), which *pleased the Jews* (Acts 12:3). Paul saw these troubles as patiently borne by the Judean Christians and those churches, including the Thessalonian church. Thus there were three models for the Thessalonians: Paul and his associates, the Lord, and the Judean churches (1 Thessalonians 1:6; 2:14).

The bitter attack on the Jews here by a man who himself was a Jew and a persecutor of Christians must be understood not as racial hostility, as if all Jews are bad people, but as a judgment of stubborn and unbelieving Jews. This kind of Jew had made life miserable for Paul, as we know from his encounters with them in many synagogues (Acts 17:5, 13; 18:5-6). That Paul deeply loved his ancestral people is clearly shown in Romans 9:1-5. He longed for and expected their ultimate salvation (Romans 9–11). But he was exasperated and pained by their present unbelief and their attempt to frustrate his ministry to the Gentiles. He saw their attitude as a continuation of the hardhearted spirit of those Jews who killed the prophets and the Lord Jesus.

These words show that Paul had very human emotions and was no plaster saint. Even Jesus said hard words about the Pharisees, lamented over the unbelief of the Galilean cities, and pronounced God's doom on them (Matthew 11:20-24; Luke 11:37-52). But neither the words of Paul nor those of Jesus should be used as an excuse to despise and condemn all Jews.

What Paul meant by *God's wrath has come upon them at last* (verse 16) is uncertain. Some scholars have contended that verses 14-16 were interpolated into this letter by someone after Paul's death and after the destruction of Jerusalem in A.D. 70, and that that judgment on the Jews is referred to here. But there is no solid evidence for this theory of interpolation. He may have meant that God's displeasure with unbelieving Jews is already being manifest in their progressive sinfulness and degradation (verse 16). The present *wrath* will soon give way to the final wrath when *God shows no partiality* (Romans 2:5-11).

§ § § § § § §

The Message of 1 Thessalonians 2:1-16

This section, particularly verses 1-12, offers a remarkable portrait of what a Christian minister should be. It should be printed and hung on the wall of every minister's study. Its applicability is obvious, but a few points may be emphasized here, most of them applying to church members as well as clergy.

§ The first is courage in the face of opposition. The courage comes from God (verse 2), not from one's own willpower. It would take unbelievable courage, after a vicious beating and imprisonment like Paul and Silas experienced at Philippi, to move just a few miles away to the next town, as the Lord had directed (Matthew 10:23), and brave the prospect of the same kind of treatment all over again. Most of us would probably head for the harbor at Neapolis and board the first ship leaving Macedonia.

§ A second point is the resolve to speak *not to please men, but to please God who tests our hearts* (verse 4). Probably the greatest temptation a minister faces today is to avoid controversial subjects and shape sermons, teaching, and comments in such a way that they will evoke assent—and better, flattering response—from hearers. This was the tactic of false preachers in Paul's time (1 Corinthians 2:1-5; 2 Corinthians 2:17; 4:2), and indeed in every time since.

§ A third point is the sharing of both the gospel and oneself (verse 8). Unfortunately, many ministers attend to a proper conceptualizing of the content of the gospel (theologizing) and to apt verbalizing of it as a pleasing context of worship and think their task well done. But, as Paul points out here, it is the gospel *incarnate in the preacher* that effects change like that described in 1:2-10. What the minister *is* is as important in transforming lives as what the minister *says*. Holy, righteous, blameless, selfless living among those we seek to help gives words divine potency. Theology and words alone are fruitless (1 Corinthians 4:19-20).

§ A fourth remark has to do with the economics of preaching. Paul and his associates went to extreme lengths to shield themselves from the charge of cupidity (greed). The trickery, flattery, and polished rhetoric of false apostles in Paul's time were aimed at what the hearers had in their pockets. Nothing much has changed. Though preaching the gospel *free of charge* (1 Corinthians 9:18) may not be possible or feasible today, the subordination of economic motives is—if transformation of the sort described in 1:2-10 is to take place in our time.

§ § § § § § §

1 Thessalonians 2:17–3:13

Introduction to These Chapters

The speedy departure by night of Paul and Silas from Thessalonica for Beroea and the subsequent flight of Paul from Beroea to Athens (Acts 17:10-15), as if they were criminals fleeing from the law and justice, were effective ammunition in the hands of Jewish enemies.

Though Silas and Timothy stayed for a while in Macedonia (Silas at Beroea and Timothy possibly at Thessalonica), they must have remained largely in hiding and have made no forward moves in the evangelizing of the province. The opposition's main fury clearly was directed against the leader of the party, Paul, though his associates cannot have escaped hostility. Paul's enemies knew that when one strikes the shepherd, it is not long before the sheep are scattered (see Mark 14:27).

On Paul's instruction, delivered by the Beroeans who escorted him to Athens, Silas and Timothy came to him there (Acts 17:15). With the success of the whole Macedonian venture at stake, Paul finally decided to send both of them back to Macedonia to do what they could to aid the new churches: Silas to Beroea and Timothy to Thessalonica. Paul remained alone in Athens (1 Thessalonians 3:1). While there he had the disastrous experience described in Acts 17:16-34.

Again frustrated, this time by cultured despisers of his curious preaching about a resurrected Jewish felon (Acts 17:31-32), he traveled westward to Corinth to attempt another mission. Undoubtedly buoyed up by living and working with a Christian couple named Aquila and Priscilla, he recovered from his loneliness and dejection (1 Corinthians 2:3) and preached persuasively in the synagogue (Acts 18:1-4).

At some point Silas and Timothy arrived in Corinth from Macedonia with good news concerning the churches there (Acts 18:5). Timothy's report about the Thessalonians (1 Thessalonians 3:6) led to Paul's writing our First Thessalonians.

This section may be divided into four parts.
I. Paul's Failure to Return (2:17-20)
II. Timothy's Mission (3:1-5)
III. Paul's Response to Timothy's Report (3:6-10)
IV. Prayer for the Thessalonians (3:11-13)

Paul's Failure to Return (2:17-20)

The heart of Paul's explanation is that his failure to return to Thessalonica was due not to lack of desire but to circumstances beyond his control. You were out of my sight but not out of my mind, he says.

Evidently his enemies in Thessalonica were telling the Christians that he had no real interest in them or he would have returned. Perhaps they said that he had found greener pastures elsewhere, something that greedy traveling preachers were always looking for.

Paul goes to considerable lengths here to emphasize his deep love of the Thessalonians. Physical separation was for him like the severing of the relationship between parent and child. Formerly he had likened the missionaries to a nursing mother (2:7), then to an exhorting, encouraging father (2:11), and now he sees himself as an orphan without them. He adds to this the statement that the separation was intended to be only *for a short time.*

Paul puts the blame for his failure to come back on Satan, not on himself. Since the accusation of indifference was made against Paul specifically (for it was he and not Silas or Timothy who had been away so long), he shifts from *we* to *I* here and practically on oath avers that he repeatedly wanted to return.

How Satan had hindered him we do not know. Was it his recurrent illness, which he regarded as an instrument of Satan to harass him (2 Corinthians 12:7)? Was it the politarchs at Thessalonica and the Jews there who were egging them on (Acts 17:5-8)? Most likely it was the bitter hostility of the Jews everywhere he had been that he had in mind, judging from his remarks about them in 2:14-16. Those who opposed the spread of the gospel could only be instruments of God's archenemy Satan! (On Satan, see the Glossary.)

The explanation of his failure to return ends with glowing assurances of the Thessalonians' value to him and his associates. *They*—not just more recent converts—are the missionaries' *hope* (of future reward at Christ's coming), their *joy* and their *crown* (the laurel wreath awarded victors in the games, worn with pride) as they stand in the presence of their glorious Lord (see 2 Corinthians 1:14).

Timothy's Mission (3:1-5)

At great sacrifice to himself, Paul sent Timothy back to Thessalonica from Athens to strengthen the Thessalonians in their time of suffering. Timothy had not yet earned the extravagant praise Paul heaped on him in his much later letter to the Philippians (2:19-22). But his emerging qualities are recognized here (verse 2).

Timothy could not roll back the suffering, but he could assist them in seeing its meaning and help them stand firm in it. To be a Christian is to experience suffering, Paul reminds them (verse 3). According to Acts 14:22 Paul told the churches at Lystra, Derbe, and Antioch that *through many hardships* (or *persecutions*) *we must enter the kingdom of God.* Had not Jesus predicted intense suffering for his disciples in the time before the end (Matthew 5:11-12; 10:16-23) and promised salvation to those who *endure to the end* (Matthew 10:22)? Paul regarded his sufferings as the mark of his authenticity as an apostle of Christ (2 Corinthians 4:7-12; 6:4-10; Galatians 6:17).

A second reason for sending Timothy was to put Paul's own mind at rest: to make sure that the *tempter* (Satan) had not used the suffering to seduce them away from their trust in and loyalty to Christ. In trial there is always the danger of falling away; so *lead us not into temptation, but deliver us from the evil one* (Matthew 6:13 and footnote; see also 1 Corinthians 10:13).

Paul's Response to Timothy's Report (3:6-10)

Paul was immensely relieved to know that the Thessalonians still held him in warm regard, longed to see him again, and were standing firm in their faith in Christ/God and love (for Paul and company and for one another). (Their problem regarding hope is taken up in 4:13-18.) It reassured him and his associates that the gospel could succeed in a hostile world. The Thessalonians' fidelity thus brought strength to the missionaries in their present distress in Corinth (verse 7; a distress perhaps referred to in Acts 18:9-17).

The absolute devotion of the missionaries to the interests of their converts is eloquently put in the statement *Now we live, if you stand firm in the Lord* (verse 8).

Verse 9 returns to the thanksgiving motif begun in 1:2, and leads on to the prayer for the readers that normally followed the thanksgiving in Paul's letters.

Prayer for the Thessalonians (3:11-13)

Verse 10 begins the reference to the prayer. The *night and day* suggests the intensity and frequency of the missionaries' prayers. It seems that set hours of prayer were inadequate for the needs and challenges they and their converts faced—that only continuous God orientation would suffice.

Paul mentions specific subjects of their prayers: the renewal of face-to-face contact with the Thessalonians so that this relationship might give opportunity to supply what was lacking in their faith; God's help in removing the obstacles that hitherto have hindered the return to Thessalonica (verse 11; 2:13); increase in the quality and extent of their love (that they may love as the missionaries love them and that their love may embrace all people, not just one another); and that the Thessalonians may be completely ready through perfection of character to stand before God at the time of the coming of the Lord Jesus.

§ § § § § § §

The Message of 1 Thessalonians 2:17–3:13

Many striking aspects of Christian faith and experience
are evident in this part of the letter.

§ *The depth of love and concern Christian leaders and laity
can have and should have for each other.*

I am an orphan without you, Paul writes. *You are our
glory and joy* and *now we live, if you stand fast in the Lord.*
We pray *night and day* for you. And on the other side, we
see the comfort that the Thessalonians' attitude toward
Paul and his associates and their constancy in the faith
gave the struggling missionaries (3:7). Soul met soul in
the Christian encounter and lives were transformed at
their deepest levels.

§ *The acceptance of suffering as normative in Christian
living and the unshakable faith that good will issue from it.*

Early Christians saw themselves as united with Christ
in his suffering and death. Suffering was not simply to be
tolerated but to be gloried in. In suffering one develops
patience and character, experiences the power of God,
bears witness to others to that enabling power, helps
carry the burdens of others, is able to comfort others with
the comfort one has received, and much more. Paul
gloried in his infirmities and weaknesses, because in
them God's *power is made perfect in weakness*
(2 Corinthians 12:9). Out of suffering with and for Christ
issues resurrection life (2 Corinthians 4:7-12, 14;
Philippians 3:10-11; 2 Timothy 2:11). In suffering *our
outer nature is wasting away,* but our inner nature is *being
renewed day by day* (2 Corinthians 4:16). Those who do not
suffer cannot be servants of a suffering Lord.

§ Evil has a power that seeks to seduce us from faith in
and loyalty to Christ and from proclaiming the gospel to
the whole world.

Paul calls this power *Satan.* Evil is that in life which

resists the loving activity of God in the universe. It has been overcome by the power of God, who acted in Christ's death and resurrection to defeat it (Romans 4:25; Colossians 2:15). By faith-identification with Christ in his death and resurrection, we can defeat evil in our lives. As Christians we must be on guard against this evil (1 Corinthians 10:12-13; 1 Thessalonians 3:5, 8).

§ Christian life begins with an initial conversion experience—a turning to God from the worship of idols, whatever they may be (1 Thessalonians 1:4-10). But this is just a beginning. There is much yet lacking. Love for other Christians and for all people, even one's enemies, must *increase and abound* (3:12 NRSV; NIV = *overflow*). We must grow into God's likeness until our whole inner self (thoughts, will, and emotions) will be transformed into readiness for life in God's presence at the coming of the Lord Jesus.

§ § § § § § §

1 Thessalonians 4

Introduction to This Chapter

The first half of Paul's letter to the Thessalonians has dealt with his and his companions' personal relationship with the Thessalonians (1:2–3:13). The second half of the letter consists of a discussion of the problems the Thessalonians have, and the way to maturity of life in Christ (4:1–5:24).

In essence, the missionaries are saying to them, Your new Christian faith and life are sound, in spite of what your enemies have charged. Now go on to maturity of life in Christ in full confidence that you are on the right track. Your Christ-taught founders (4:1-2) and your own leaders (5:12) will help you along the way, and God will make you completely holy (5:24). You can and will come out blameless in character and life at the time of Christ's coming (3:13; 5:23). And, together with your Christian dead (4:13-18), you will participate in life in the presence of the Lord (4:17; 5:9-10).

The problems Paul deals with here were suggested by Timothy, who had just returned from Thessalonica, and also may have been raised in a letter Timothy seems to have brought from the church there. Note the word *about* (NIV; NRSV = *concerning* in 4:9, 13; 5:1, by which Paul introduced matters about which the Corinthians wrote him (1 Corinthians 7:1, 25; 8:1; 12:1).

This section may be outlined as follows.

Personal Sexual Morality (4:1-8)

A general exhortation to remember and follow what Paul and his companions already had told them about the moral requirements of Christian faith and life introduces the new section (4:1-2).

Paul's gospel apparently included considerably more than only the preaching of Christ crucified (1 Corinthians 2:2). It included the meaning of his life, death, and resurrection for life in this world, as all of his letters show, mostly in their latter parts.

Here (verses 1 and 2) Paul cites the Lord Jesus as the authority for his instructions. Exactly how the Lord Jesus stands behind them he does not say. Whether he knew a collection of Jesus' teachings, handed down in the church, with which he regarded his instruction as in agreement, or whether he is referring to instructions given to him and his associates by the indwelling Christ (the Holy Spirit) is not clear. But the fact that he seems to refer to pre-Resurrection words of the Lord in 1 Corinthians 7:10-11, 25; 9:14; and 11:23-25 favors the view that he has in mind the actual historical teaching of Jesus.

As authority for his views he also alludes to or cites Scripture (Romans 12:19-20; 1 Corinthians 5:7-8; 6:16), appeals to accepted church practice (1 Corinthians 11:2, 16; 2 Thessalonians 2:15), and offers his own *trustworthy* opinion (1 Corinthians 7:25). The hub of his ethical instruction is the same as that of Jesus: love for God and neighbor (Mark 12:29-31; Romans 13:8-10). *Let all that you do be done in love* (1 Corinthians 16:14), he writes.

The first problem discussed here has to do with sexual relationships. Attitudes toward sex in Hellenistic religion and life were very liberal in comparison with standards in Judaism and Christianity. Jesus' teaching about sex and relationships was even more stringent than in Judaism. For him the lustful, adulterous desire was as culpable as the adulterous act (Matthew 5:27-28). In Pharisaic Judaism divorce of one's wife was granted even for trivial reasons. In contrast, Jesus held that permanence in marriage was God's intention (Mark 10:2-9).

Paul did his best to hold marriages together in his churches (1 Corinthians 7:10-16) and to promote high moral standards among the unmarried and the married. He was horrified about a case of incest in the Corinthian church (1 Corinthians 5:1-5) and about members of that church who patronized prostitutes (1 Corinthians 6:15-20). He believed that God has a will for human beings in sexual matters (1 Thessalonians 4:3-8), and that what Christians do with their bodies is important. They are temples of the Holy Spirit, in an exclusive relationship with Christ, and destined to experience a resurrection like his (1 Corinthians 6:13-20).

God's will is *sanctification* (verse 3). This word signifies separation from all that is unclean, complete dedication to God, and growing Godlikeness. Sexual immorality is contrary to God's will and will bring down divine judgment on guilty persons (verse 6).

What Paul specifically asks for here is not clear. The NIV and NRSV have *how to take a wife*; NRSV; *learn to live with his own wife*, NIV). *how to control his own body*, with a footnote suggesting as an alternative translation. The problem is the meaning here of a Greek word literally translated *vessel*. Is the vessel a wife or one's own body? Scholars are divided. If Paul means mastery over his body, then the Thessalonians are asked to honor that body and not devote it to lustful relationships like pagans who are ignorant of God. Respect for the body, for its union with Christ, and for its destiny was important to Paul, as we saw above.

If a wife is meant, the statement stresses the importance of pure and honorable marriage, not the entering into lustful relationships outside marriage as pagans do. Thus unchastity (sexual immorality)—an impediment to sanctification (Godlikeness)—will be checked in the church.

A difficulty appears also in verse 6. Is adultery with a brother's wife opposed here? Or is greed in business being spoken against? (See the NRSV footnote.) Covetousness is often mentioned along with sexual immorality in the New Testament. But the context deals with sexual sins, not money and business. And the word *impure* in verse 7 seems still to have sexual irregularities in view.

Paul's view of sex, as a whole, included the importance of marriage itself, fidelity and respect for one's partner within marriage, self-control and chastity outside of marriage, and the permanence of marriage (though he admits that this goal may not always be possible— 1 Corinthians 7:15).

At the end of the discussion here of personal sexual morality, Paul says that the Christian who rejects God's call to purity in sexual matters is rejecting not human, but rather divine authority and affronting the indwelling Holy Spirit (verse 8).

Love and Work in the Community (4:9-12)

Love of fellow believers was a mark of early Christianity (John 15:12; Romans 12:10). The Macedonian churches excelled in it, as illustrated by their generous contribution to Paul's collection for the Jerusalem church (2 Corinthians 8:1-5).

Here the Thessalonians are praised for their love for Christians throughout Macedonia and urged to continue and expand it (verse 10). How this love was expressed we do not know. But that it was practical help (charitable gifts? hospitality to strangers? supplying of personnel? moral support?) seems probable. In this generosity they were God-taught, evidently by the Holy Spirit within them.

But not all of the Thessalonian Christians were contributing their share to the Christian community at Thessalonica and to other Christians in Macedonia. Some were lazy spongers, agitators, and busybodies. They were giving the church a bad reputation with pagans. Paul rebukes them here and even more vehemently in 2 Thessalonians 3:6-13. Perhaps the letter Timothy seems to have brought to Paul from the Thessalonians asked for directions for dealing with these troublesome loafers.

Destiny of the Christian Dead (4:13-18)

Another problem bothering the Thessalonians, and possibly inquired about in the letter Timothy brought to Paul, concerned the destiny of Christians who died before the final coming of Christ. Would they miss out on the glorious Kingdom Christ will inaugurate at his coming? (Paul treats other questions concerning Christ's coming in 5:1-11 and in 2 Thessalonians.)

Paul says that the Thessalonian dead are *asleep* (NIV; NRSV = *dead*). *Asleep* was a common euphemism for *dead* in both Judaism and Hellenism (1 Kings 2:10; 11:43). This metaphor arose from the obvious likeness between death and sleep. It is found frequently in the New Testament (John 11:11-13; 1 Corinthians 15:6, 18; 2 Peter 3:4). For Christians it is an apt metaphor in view of the Christian hope, referred to here (verse 13), of the awakening of Christians through the resurrected Jesus (verse 14).

When he discussed at Thessalonica the coming of Christ and the participation of Christians in his future Kingdom, Paul apparently had said nothing about the status of Christians who might die before the great event. He had presented this event as near at hand (see Romans

13:11-14; 1 Corinthians 7:29-31; Philippians 4:5; and the phrases in verses 15 and 17 here, *we who are alive, who are left until the coming of the Lord*). Some church members had died since he left Thessalonica and the question of their relation to the coming Kingdom naturally arose.

Paul's answer is brief and clear cut. They will not be left out. When the Lord comes in glorious pageantry to claim his own, *the dead in Christ will rise first* and the living will *be caught up together with them in the clouds to meet the Lord in the air* and to enjoy together and forever the Lord's companionship. The heart of Paul's hope for the future was to be with the Lord always (5:10; 2 Corinthians 5:6-9).

The nature of Paul's view of the coming of Christ will be discussed in some fullness in our consideration of his second letter to the Thessalonians.

§ § § § § § §

The Message of 1 Thessalonians 4

Paul's teachings about sex, love of fellow believers, and faithful work for the good of oneself and the community present clear challenges to the church of our time. Here are a few brief remarks about his view of the coming of Christ.

§ Paul employs here the picturesque metaphors and symbols of Jewish-Christian apocalyptic (see the Glossary): the cry of command, the archangel's call; the trumpet of God; the clouds; the air. Like the language of the books of Daniel and Revelation (the beasts, the trumpets, the bowls, the thrones, the sea of glass, angels and living creatures, a great harlot), Paul's picture of the coming of Christ must be taken as a metaphorical characterization of what cannot be accurately described.

§ Paul's belief that the coming of Christ would occur in his generation matches that of Jesus himself (Mark 9:1; 13:28-30). But neither would predict the exact time; both left the time of the coming to God's authority and decision (Mark 13:32; Acts 1:7; 2 Thessalonians 2:1-12).

Jesus even suggested that God might extend the period of grace before Christ's coming (Mark 13:20; Luke 13:6-9; 18:7). God's will is not unalterable, but depends on the character of our response (see Jeremiah 18:7-10). Therefore, the time of the end cannot be predicted. Paul saw a God-ordained restrainer at work, giving opportunity for the spread of the gospel (2 Thessalonians 2:6-7).

Both Jesus and Paul stressed the importance of preparedness for that great event (Matthew 24:42-51; 25:1-13; Romans 13:11-14; 1 Thessalonians 5:1-11). Since God gives people a period of grace, they must seize the opportunity for preparation (by repentance, renewal, diligent proclamation of the gospel, and Christlike living). They are not to usurp God's authority over times and dates (Acts 1:7).

§ The catching up of dead and living Christians to meet Christ in the air cannot properly be used to form a doctrine of "the Rapture" (rescue) of the saints to shield them from a seven-year period of tribulation, as is so often claimed. In the Book of Revelation the saints are pictured as going through the end time tribulations (Revelation 2:10; 6:9-11; 17:6; 18:24; 19:2), not as being rescued from them. And neither here nor in Matthew 24:40-41 is there any suggestion of an ongoing earthly order while the righteous are away *in the air*. Both Jesus and Paul contemplate the end of the earthly process at the coming of Christ for his final judgment of all people; and they seem to expect thereafter the eternal, heavenly kingdom of God.

§ § § § § § §

1 Thessalonians 5

Introduction to This Chapter

Paul's teaching at Thessalonica obviously gave a large place to instruction about the coming of the Lord. But on three points he had not been explicit enough: what would happen to church members who might die before the great event (4:13-18); exactly when it would happen (5:2-3); and what style of life would be appropriate in the meantime (5:4-11).

Paul seems to have thought he had given them adequate instruction on the second and third of these questions (5:1), but Timothy's report and perhaps inquiries in a letter he brought to Paul indicated clearly that he had not done so, or that they had not comprehended what he had said.

Paul's response here about the time of the coming of the day of the Lord points out its suddenness and unpredictability (5:2-3).

Paul uses several terms for the great end time event: *the revealing* of the Lord Jesus Christ (1 Corinthians 1:7); his *coming* (literally, his presence—1 Corinthians 15:23; 1 Thessalonians 2:19; 2 Thessalonians 2:1, 8); his *appearing* (2 Thessalonians 2:8); and *the day of our Lord Jesus Christ* or *Christ* (1 Corinthians 1:8; 5:5; 2 Corinthians 1:14; Philippians 2:16; 1 Thessalonians 5:2). Neither Paul nor other New Testament writers use the term *second coming*, though Hebrews 9:28 comes close to it. *Second coming* goes back to Justin Martyr in the second century.

As a phrase signifying the end event, *the day of the Lord* reaches back as far as Amos (eighth century B.C.; see Amos 5:18). In the Old Testament and in Jewish usage it meant the day of God, when God would judge the people and the world and inaugurate the new kingdom. When Jesus became *Lord* to the church, aspects of the work of God were transferred to him.

This section has four main parts.
I. The Times and the Seasons (5:1-3)
II. While Christians Await the Day (5:4-11)
III. Counsels for Church Life and Worship (5:12-24)
IV. The Conclusion (5:25-28)

The Times and the Seasons (5:1-3)

This phrase stems from the Old Testament (Daniel 2:21; 7:12) and became traditional for the period of divine intervention in human events predetermined by God (Acts 1:7). Many Jewish writings of the time of Jesus and Paul laid stress on knowledge about these times.

By using two figures of speech here (the thief in the night and the woman in labor) Paul stresses the suddenness and unpredictability of Christ's coming. Both figures were used before Paul: the thief in the night by Jesus (Matthew 24:43-44; Luke 12:39-40); and the woman in labor by Isaiah (13:6-8). The sudden arrival of *the day* will surprise those who feel themselves secure and comfortable. (See also Luke 17:20-37.)

While Christians Await the Day (5:4-11)

Four suggestions are offered to the Thessalonians here for life in the waiting period.

(1) *Remember who and what you are. You are all sons of light* (NIV; NRSV = *children of*) *and sons of the day* and *not of the night or of darkness* (5:5).

The *all* evidently includes those tempted to live unchastely (4:2-8, possibly *the weak* of 5:14), the agitators, busybodies, and idlers (4:11-12; 5:14), those worried about their dead loved ones (4:13-18, possibly *the fainthearted* of 5:14), and those who have been upset doctrinally and emotionally by their Jewish opponents (chapters 1–3).

The whole church is *in God the Father and the Lord Jesus Christ* (1:1). They are God's chosen people (1:4), filled with God's spirit (1:6), transformed from idol worship to fellowship with and service of the living God (1:9), imitators of the Judean churches in suffering for Christ (2:14), the missionaries' *glory and joy* (2:20). Since they are God's own people, not one of them needs to be lost. The God who called them will see to it that they are wholly set apart and prepared completely for the coming of the Lord Jesus Christ (5:23). God is reliable (5:24). Have no fear!

In Semitic idiom *son of* (NIV; NRSV = *children*) expresses affinity or likeness. To embody and express the quality of a thing was to be a son of that thing. Thus a son of light, a son of the day, a son of peace, a son of thunder, or a son of Gehenna is one who embodies and expresses these qualities in his character and life; he is the offspring of them, as it were.

Light (day) in a moral sense (meaning goodness and well-being, both present and future) comprised the essential nature and way of living of the Thessalonian Christians, whereas *darkness* or *night* (meaning evil and disaster, present and future) was characteristic of pagans.

The Essenes, who gave us the Dead Sea Scrolls, called themselves "the sons of light" and called outsiders "the sons of darkness." They too believed themselves headed for a kingdom of light, as did Christians (John 8:12; Colossians 1:12-13; Revelation 21:23-25).

(2) *Keep awake and be sober* (5:6 [NRSV; NIV = *be alert and self-controlled*]).

Sleep here is what creatures of darkness do. They are

not awake to the glorious possibilities of life in Christ here and hereafter, and they are morally careless.

Keep awake, literally *watch*, so you will not be taken by surprise by the Lord's coming for salvation and judgment, was often on the lips of Jesus (Matthew 24:42-44; 25:13; Mark 13:35-37).

Sober here, while it signifies the opposite of alcoholic drunkenness, as 5:7 shows, means basically well-balanced and self-controlled.

(3) *Put on God's armor* (5:8).

Christians will need God's armor to overcome the forces of evil in the waiting period. Here the famous triad *faith, love,* and *hope* appears again (1:3; Romans 5:1-5; 1 Corinthians 13:13; Galatians 5:5-6; Colossians 1:4-5). On the Christian armor see Ephesians 6:11-17 and its predecessor in the Old Testament (Isaiah 59:17).

(4) *Keep in mind your destiny* (5:9-10).

Their destiny is not *wrath* (God's/Christ's condemnation at the Day of Judgment—1:10; 2 Corinthians 5:10) but *salvation* (health, well-being, beginning now and continuing into life in the kingdom of God). Salvation is made possible through the death of the Lord Jesus Christ. The essence of salvation is life with Christ (5:10).

(5) *Encourage one another and build up one another* (5:11).

This is the function of all church members, not just the leadership (1 Corinthians 14:31; Ephesians 4:7-16).

Counsels for Church Life and Worship (5:12-24)

In general, the counsels are quite clear and need little explanation. Only a few points will be commented on.

The admonition *Do not quench the Spirit* (5:19 NRSV) considers the Spirit to be a flame of fire (Acts 2:3). Paul is referring in these words to the Spirit's manifestations (gifts), as the reference to prophesying (5:20) shows.

Apparently there were some at Thessalonica who despised these manifestations (*prophesying*—speaking in tongues? healings and miracles of various sorts?). Paul believed that the Spirit's manifestations (even tongues, under proper restraints in public worship and when interpreted—1 Corinthians 14:13-19, 27) have edifying value and should not be stifled. Here, as in 1 Corinthians 14, he places prophesying (readily intelligible communication between speaker and hearer in which the will of God is declared—not just the predicting of future events) as of central importance. He asks also for discrimination in regard to the gifts and their use. He stresses here, as in 1 Corinthians 14:13-20, the importance of the mind in Christian life and worship.

Paul's wishful prayer for the complete sanctification of the Thessalonians (5:23) matches the prayer for their holiness with which the second part of the letter was introduced (3:11-13). The call to sanctification (holiness) appears again in 4:3, 4, 7. In fact, this whole part of the letter deals with how holiness or sanctification (both Greek words thus translated in English have behind them the same Greek root) may be obtained. Sanctification (being set apart *from* everything that is profane and unclean and *to* a life that is pleasing to God) is both God's will (4:2) and God's work (5:23-24). What it involves in practical terms will be pointed out below under "The Message of 1 Thessalonians 5."

The Conclusion (5:25-28)

The closing words are meant to strengthen the bonds of fellowship between Paul and the Thessalonians and to promote good relationships within the church there. The tender *pray for us* would leave the Thessalonians with the feeling that Paul needs them as much as they need him. The injunction to greet *believers* with a *holy kiss* suggests that the fellowship may have been fractured by the attitudes and conduct of some. The church meeting at which Paul's letter was to be read would further cement the group and its loyalty to Paul. God is a *God of peace*

(5:23) and wills peace and unity among the chosen people (5:12-13).

§ § § § § § §

The Message of 1 Thessalonians 5

§ What sanctification (holiness) means in practical terms is spelled out by Paul in chapters 4 and 5.

§ In general terms, it is the process and state of Christian maturity that should follow from the Holy Spirit's work in conversion (1:5-6). It is increasing and abounding in love to one another (3:12). It is *a life worthy of God* (2:12), a life characterized by the kind of blamelessness that can stand the test of Christ's judgment at the time of Christ's coming (1:10; 3:13; 4:6; 5:2-3, 9).

§ In specific terms, both attitudes and conduct are included. Christian maturity (holiness, sanctification) embraces all that Paul has included in the latter half of his letter: sexual purity, brotherly love (mutual helpfulness and unstinting forgiveness), quiet minding of one's own business, industriousness, mature theological understanding of the Christian situation in the time before the End, spiritual alertness and self-control, respect for church leaders, thankfulness and prayerfulness, gratitude for and effective use of the Holy Spirit's gifts, the ability to discriminate between right and wrong, and power to reject evil and do what is good. All this Paul includes under the category of holiness.

§ For Paul, holy persons are not pallid, ascetic recluses who specialize in vague, rapturous inner experiences. Rather, they are persons whose total attitudes and way of life are shaped by the God who dwells in them as the Holy Spirit (4:8). This quality of life is God's gift to those who seek *more and more* to please God (4:1).

§ § § § § § §

Introduction to 2 Thessalonians

On the church at Thessalonica and the problems addressed by Paul in 1 Thessalonians, see the Introduction to 1 Thessalonians, pages 105-7.

The Occasion and Purpose of the Letter

The letter indicates that reports had come to Paul about problems in the church at Thessalonica (3:11) mainly concerning the persecution the church was experiencing, probably from both Jews and Gentiles (1:4-8).

Another problem centered in wrong ideas some Thessalonians had about the coming of Christ. Someone evidently claimed Paul as the authority for the false view that *the day of the Lord has already come* (2:2). The practical result of this mistaken view was that some people had quit their daily work. Thus there was a great deal of idleness and meddling in other people's affairs (3:6, 11). Paul had faced the problem of lazy spongers when he was at Thessalonica (3:10), but his instructions went unheeded. Indeed, the situation was much worse.

We can only guess who was teaching church members at Thessalonica that the day of the Lord had arrived.

There were church members at Corinth who believed that they were enjoying the kingdom of God already (1 Corinthians 4:8). A clear statement in 2 Timothy 2:18 attributes to two false teachers in the church the view that the resurrection is already past. Such a position was held by Gnostic heretics (see the Glossary) of the late first and second centuries, and may have appeared in embryonic form in the church as early as the time of Paul. It held that the only resurrection there ever will be is release of the spirit from the bondage of flesh, which occurs in baptism and new birth.

Or had the Thessalonians taken too realistically Paul's statement in 1 Thessalonians 5:5, 8 that they were *sons of* (NIV; NRSV = *children of*) *the day* and *we belong to the day*, as if the day had already broken in? In addition, did the severity of suffering suggest to them that the end-time birth pangs of the new order (see Isaiah 66:7-9) were actually being felt?

It is even possible that a forged letter, claiming Paul's authorship and authority for the view that the day of the Lord had arrived, was circulating at Thessalonica (2:2). Such a letter would make necessary Paul's repudiation of it and the reference to his handwriting as a way of authenticating his letters in the future (3:17).

Whatever the exact cause of the confusion, Paul felt it important to straighten out the Thessalonians on the significance, time, and consequence of the coming of Christ for present living.

Authorship, Date, and Place of Writing

It is difficult to explain why we have two letters to the Thessalonians that are so alike and yet so different.

Second Thessalonians covers many of the same subjects as First Thessalonians: notably, thanksgiving for the readers' steadfastness in persecution; a declaration of God's judgment on their persecutors; prayers for their establishment in every good work and word (2 Thessalonians 2:17); teaching about End events (eschatology; see the Glossary) and about appropriate Christian conduct in the time before the End; and emphasis on Paul's and his associates' authority and on traditional church teaching. And much of the language and phraseology is the same in the two letters.

But there are marked differences. First Thessalonians is warm in tone and filled with personal data; 2 Thessalonians is colder, more formal, and authoritarian. The first letter stresses the unpredictability and suddenness of the coming of Christ; the second offers signs by which one can predict that coming. The second gives information about *the lawless one*—a kind of speculation about the future that is unparalleled anywhere in the letters of Paul.

Under what circumstances would Paul and his associates write two letters to the Thessalonians so alike, so different, and so close together in time?

Many scholars believe that within a few months of the writing of 1Thessalonians the missionaries, then at Corinth, received new reports about the situation at Thessalonica (2 Thessalonians 3:11). The church members there had not wavered in loyalty to Christ because of persecutions and afflictions (1:4). But serious controversy about the time of the coming of Christ had arisen, provoked by revelations claimed by false teachers and possibly by a letter falsely attributed to Paul. The false teaching that the day of the Lord had already come had led to serious moral consequences in the church. The missionaries wrote to correct the new situation, which was yet not wholly new. Therefore the similarities and differences in the two letters. The date of writing of Second Thessalonians then would be A.D. 50 or 51.

Other scholars believe that a disciple of Paul (perhaps between A.D. 75 and 90) used 1 Thessalonians as a source of material for a rebuttal of the claim made in the Christian church of that time that Paul believed that the day of the Lord had already arrived. This rebuttal is our Second Thessalonians. Because of his imitation of Paul's language and ideas, the letters are similar; and, because of his later date, situation, and purpose the letters are different.

The most satisfactory view is probably the first.

2 Thessalonians 1:1–3:18

Introduction to These Chapters

The letter follows the usual outline employed in Paul's letters. The parts need no special treatment here. We shall follow the development of thought, however.

Second Thessalonians has three main parts.
  I. Introduction (1:1-4)
 II. God's Righteous Judgment (1:5-10)
III. The Coming of Christ (2:1-14)
 IV. Paul's View of Last Things (2:15–3:18)

Introduction (1:1-4)

The discussion of the coming of Christ begins from the situation of the Christians at Thessalonica. They were experiencing bitter persecution. Paul praises them for their steadfastness and continued growth in faith and love. He insists on doing so, in spite of their objection that they are unworthy of such praise (1:3).

God's Righteous Judgment (1:5-10)

Paul regards the patient endurance of persecution as proof of God's righteous (right, just) judgment. This judgment is seen now in God's support of the suffering Christians while they are being prepared through their suffering for membership in the coming Kingdom. It will be fully seen at the glorious coming of the Lord Jesus, when recompense will be meted out to the afflicted and to their tormentors (1:5-10).

The reward for the persecuted Christians will be *rest* (relief from trouble and suffering) and eternal fellowship with the Lord, while the recompense of the wicked will be trouble and eternal ruin, that is, separation from the presence of the glorious and mighty Lord (1:7, 9).

The Coming of Christ (2:1-14)

Following the discussion of the coming of Christ at the day of recompense, Paul turns to the time of the coming (2:1-12). Here he deals with the error that the day of the Lord has already come by showing that the preliminary events of the divine timetable have not yet run their course.

Christ will not come until the self-deifying *lawless one* appears. This one will come as the human incarnation of all evil. He will deceive people by Satanic power and induce them to false worship. Christ will appear to destroy this devil's messiah and to render judgment on his unrighteous worshipers. Paul says that a mysterious force of lawlessness is now at work in the world, but the coming of the lawless one is being held back by something or someone—what or who the Thessalonians are said to know and are not told again here (2:5-6).

Who *the lawless one* is and what or who the restrainer is elude us. Was some Gentile or Jewish leader, someone like Antiochus Epiphanes or the mad emperor Gaius (Caligula), expected to appear as the embodiment of all evil and as the devil's instrument in the final great struggle between the forces of good and evil at the end of time? It is unlikely that Paul had some specific historical person in mind.

Some guesses about the identity of the restrainer are: the Roman empire (and the emperor), which held back the surge of lawlessness; an angel, perhaps Michael; the

Holy Spirit; Paul and the proclamation of the gospel to the Gentiles. Speculation is useless.

The main point is that God's calendar of historical events has not yet been fulfilled and, until it is, the end of the age and the coming of the kingdom of God—to be introduced by the return of Christ—cannot take place. The Gnostic heretics, who claim that salvation has been *fully* realized in the resurrection and liberation of the self from the bondage of matter, are wrong. Salvation, whatever its present aspects (and these are not treated in this letter), is emphatically God's *future* gift (2:10, 13-14).

While Christians await the coming of Christ and the salvation to be bestowed in the gift of life in God's kingdom, they must be obedient to the pattern of doctrine and living taught them by Paul and his associates (2:15; 3:4, 6-12). This means a life of good works and words (2:17)—not idleness and gossip and troublemaking, but the Christian activities of prayer (3:1), personal industriousness (3:6-12), and tireless well-doing (3:13).

Paul's View of Last Things (2:15–3:18)

Paul's hope for the future, as that of the early church as a whole, rested on the belief of Old Testament writers that God had promised patriarchs and prophets a glorious Kingdom in which God and the chosen people would dwell together forever. This hope took three forms in the course of Israel's history.

(1) There was the hope for the coming of a glorified earthly order, under a God-appointed human leader, marked by universal worship of and loyalty to God, political stability and peace, social felicity, and economic abundance.

(2) When pessimism grew up about the earth as a fit place for the eternal dwelling-place of God and humankind, the new order was conceived of as a

heavenly dwelling without finite limitation, to be governed by a supernatural being, the Son of man.

(3) A third form consisted of the combination of the above: first an earthly order (sometimes conceived of as 40, 60, 400, 1,000, or more years), ruled by a human messiah, and then the heavenly eternal order, ruled by God.

The Revelation to John in the New Testament contains the combination form (20:4–22:5), though it is not clear that the millennial Kingdom is really thought of as an earthly order. (It may be a symbol by which John refers to the reign of Christ in the world since Easter.) No New Testament person or writer conceives of the coming Kingdom as an eternal *earthly* order.

While Paul mentions Christ as reigning until he has defeated his enemies (1 Corinthians 15:25), no earthly interim order is mentioned. Paul clearly believed the coming of Christ would result in the resurrection of dead Christians and the transformation into a heavenly form of being for living Christians (1 Thessalonians 4:16-17; 1 Corinthians 15:51-52). The coming Kingdom would be a heavenly, not an earthly, abode (2 Corinthians 5:1-5). Jesus appears also to have believed this (Mark 12:25; Luke 20:34-36). The concept of an earthly millennium has scant support in the New Testament.

In a sense, however, Jesus, Paul, and the church believed that the kingdom of God was present in the world before its coming in glory. The Messiah had appeared in the person of Jesus. In and through him the power of the coming Kingdom was operating in this world (Luke 7:21-22; 11:20). And by his resurrection from the dead the first act in the eschatological drama had occurred (1 Corinthians 15:20-23). The Holy Spirit, the gift of the resurrected Jesus, dwelt in persons and the church as the *guarantee* (that is, down payment) of their life in the coming Kingdom (2 Corinthians 1:22; 5:5; Ephesians 1:14). The coming age had overlapped the present age. The church was the coming Kingdom in outpost. There was a joyful sense of present realization of the kingdom of God that Judaism knew nothing of.

However, the church (and to some degree Jesus—Mark 13:5-22) believed that preceding the coming of Christ (the Son of man) with the final Kingdom the church would experience a time of great testing and suffering. This age would be instigated by false Christs, false prophets, and a diabolical tyrant—the *lawless one* (the Antichrist)—who would deceive even the elect (2 Thessalonians 2:3-12). This lawless one was apparently modeled after the figure of the self-deifying tyrants Antiochus IV ("Epiphanes") and the Emperor Gaius (Caligula). By fidelity even to death, if need be, the righteous would be purged and would attain eternal life in the coming Kingdom (Revelation 2:10; 7:9-17). The church could not escape this time of suffering, but must go steadfastly through it (Acts 14:22; 1 Thessalonians 3:3-4). Paul prayed that he might present his converts unblamable in holiness before God and the coming Lord (1 Thessalonians 3:13; 5:23).

Exactly when the Lord would come Jesus, Paul, and the church did not know (Mark 13:32; Acts 1:7). Both Jesus and Paul seem to have thought it would happen during their generation (Matthew 10:23; Mark 9:1; 13:30; 1 Corinthians 7:29-31; 1 Thessalonians 4:15). But both believed that some events would occur first (the fall of Jerusalem, Luke 21:20-24; the universal proclamation of the gospel, Mark 13:10 and scattered hints in Paul's letters; the time of testing of the saints, as indicated above). They were content to leave the exact time to God, anxious only, along with their converts, to be alert, active in the tasks committed to them, patient, and morally spotless in the time remaining.

This is unquestionably the proper attitude and life-style for Christians of every generation.

§ § § § § § §

The Message of 2 Thessalonians 1:1-3:18

§ God has a glorious Kingdom in store for the people called through Christ Jesus and the gospel (2:13-14).

§ Christian suffering is a means by which God's people become worthy of the kingdom of God (1:5, 11). In suffering, faith, steadfastness, and love they are perfected (1:3-4; 3:5).

§ The power of evil (Satan) will be with us to the end, but will ultimately be defeated by the victorious Christ (2:3-8). Evil is a terrifying reality in life. It becomes incarnate in diabolical persons, who lead unrighteous unbelievers into strong delusion and hostility to the truth (2:9-12). Christians can triumph over that power if they pray for one another, persevere in the faith, and do what is right (3:1-5).

§ The recompense to be meted out to doers of evil is separation from the presence of God and *from the glory of his might* (1:9 [NRSV; NIV = *majesty of his power*]), really the continuation of the separation they had brought about by their own unbelief and evil deeds. Here *eternal destruction* is defined as exclusion from God who is the giver of life. The recompense of the righteous is *rest* (relief, as of the relaxation of a taut bowstring—1:7) and life in the presence of the glorious Lord.

§ Christian life in this world anticipates the life of the final kingdom of God. God has more in store for us than we have yet realized. While we are *sons of the day*, the day has not yet arrived in all its glory (2:2). Meanwhile, we wait in patience for the fulfilling of God's final purpose.

§ Life's responsibilities need to be carried out faithfully while we await the great finale. Laziness, idleness, sponging on others, and meddling in the affairs of others bring no credit to the church before the world

(2 Thessalonians 3:6-12; 1 Thessalonians 4:11-12). The church should discipline such people in love (2 Thessalonians 3:6, 14-15).

§ § § § § § §

Glossary of Terms

Aegean Sea: The body of water leading from the Mediterranean Sea to the Black Sea and washing the shores of Turkey (the Roman province of Asia) on the east, Greece on the west, and Macedonia on the north. It was crossed several times by Paul.

Antichrist: A term appearing in the New Testament only in Second and Third John for the final, Satan-backed opponent (or opponents) of Christ. Paul refers to him as *the man of lawlessness* or *the lawless one* (2 Thessalonians 2:3, 8), whom Christ will destroy at his final advent. Prototypes of this figure are Gog (Ezekiel 38–39), Antiochus IV (Epiphanes—see below), and Belial (in several books of the intertestamental period.)

Antiochus IV (Epiphanes—"the God manifest"): A fanatical Syrian king (175-163 B.C.), who sought to force Greek culture and religion on the Jews, defiled their Temple in Jerusalem, and provoked the Maccabean rebellion.

Apocalyptic: From a Greek word meaning "the unveiling of something hidden," especially of God's hidden purposes for the world, which have been revealed to special persons. The books in which the disclosures are described are called *apocalypses.*

Apostle: From a Greek word meaning "one who is sent out" as the commissioned representative of another. In the New Testament it usually designates a person who belonged to the inner circles of Jesus' followers (the Twelve) and who was an eyewitness of the first events and an official representative of Jesus. Later it was broadened to include Paul and others who were especially commissioned by Jesus Christ (Acts 14:14; Romans 16:7; 1 Corinthians 9:1).

Caligula: Gaius, great-nephew of the Emperor Tiberius, nicknamed *Caligula,* was Roman emperor from A.D. 37 to 41. He believed he was the incarnation of Jupiter and demanded that his statue be worshiped. He appointed Herod Agrippa king in Palestine.

Chiasmus: A form of poetic structure in which words or lines are mentioned in one sequence like ascending stairs and are reversed in order in the following sequence like descending stairs (for example, Isaiah 6:10).

Day of the Lord: From the time of Amos (8th century B.C.) on, it meant the great day when God would judge the world (both Israel and the nations) and inaugurate the new Kingdom (see Amos 5:18-20; Joel 2:30-31). In the New Testament *the Lord* is the returning Jesus (1 Corinthians 1:8).

Dead Sea Scrolls: Documents discovered (beginning in 1947) in caves by the Dead Sea, deposited there by members of a Jewish monastic community (probably Essenes) that existed there from about the middle of the second century B.C. until about A.D. 70.

Divine Men: Roving teachers, some within the Christian church, around the time of Paul, who claimed to be incarnations of a god or god-filled, to possess divine knowledge about the universe and the way of salvation, and to have miraculous powers of perception, speech, and healing. Paul opposed such teachers in his letters to the Corinthians, the Colossians, and the Thessalonians.

Eschatology: An aspect of theology, dealing with last things, the meaning of one element of the underlying Greek term. It is concerned with the consummation of history and what lies beyond history.

Essenes: One of the four Jewish sects identified by Josephus, the others being the Pharisees, the Sadducees, and the Zealots. They were strict observers of the laws of Moses, were preoccupied with their special place as the end-time people of God, and were probably the writers of the Dead Sea Scrolls at Qumran by the Dead Sea.

Freedmen: Slaves in the Greco-Roman world who had secured their freedom by purchase or by working to achieve it.

Gnosticism and Gnostics: A system of thought and its advocates who offered escape for the divine/human spirit of people from the oppressive bondage of evil flesh through enlightenment, often brought by a redeemer figure. Gnostics, holding that the flesh was evil, either denied its drives and became ascetics or gave the flesh free reign and became libertines. They seem to have upset several Pauline churches (at Corinth, Thessalonica, and Colossae) and to have drawn Paul's unsparing condemnation.

God-fearers: Gentiles, male and female, who were attracted to Jewish synagogue worship by its monotheism and high spiritual and moral qualities but who did not want to accept the full yoke of the Jewish law (circumcision, food laws, and sabbath observance). Paul had large success with this group of Gentiles.

Hellenism: The Roman Empire was deeply shaped by Greek culture throughout its existence.

Hellenistic: An adjective used to characterize a cultural period reaching in Palestine from the conquests of Alexander the Great (336-323 B.C.) to the beginning of the Roman Period (63 B.C.).

Holiness: A state of relationship to God in which a person or thing is separated from all that is profane and unclean, completely dedicated to God, and suitable for association with God.

Logos: The Greek term for *word*. In Greek philosophical thought it referred to the principle of rationality behind the universe by which the universe is ordered and sustained. In the Prologue of the Gospel of John the *Logos* is the mode of the divine creativity and revelation.

Messiah: A Hebrew title meaning *the anointed one.* Originally applied to kings and prophets, in late periods of Israel's history it was used as a designation of a coming end-time deliverer who would deliver God's people from their enemies and introduce the kingdom of God.

Michael: Israel's patron angel (Daniel 10:13, 21; 12:1), who fights for righteous Israel against the opposing angels of evil powers. In some intertestamental literature he will lead the heavenly hosts in the final battle against the forces of evil.

Millennium: A thousand-year period of peace and blessedness for the earth, believed by late Jewish and Christian writers to be near at hand. See Revelation 20:1-6.

Mystery Cults: Religions of the late Hellenistic Age (100 B.C.-A.D. 300) that promised union with various deities and eternal life through secret knowledge and rites of initiation.

Plato and Platonic: A fourth century B.C. Greek philosopher, whose students and their successors created a philosophical system widely popular in the Hellenistic and Roman periods. Plato-like views influenced some early Christian writers.

Politarchs: In Macedonia the politarchs were the local, non-Roman magistrates of a free city, who were the instruments of Rome in maintaining law and order.

Praetorium: Either the place of residence of the Roman emperor's large and elite bodyguard or the palace of the emperor, a Roman governor, or a client king in outlying areas.

Proconsul: A former Roman consul who served as the governor of a province or in command of a Roman army.

Proselytes: Gentile converts to Judaism. Full acceptance of

Jewish law and ritual practices were required, as if the converts had been born Jews.

Qumran Texts: Qumran is the Arabic name of the place where the Dead Sea Scrolls and a monastery (probably Essene) were discovered after 1947.

Right Teacher: The founder or organizing genius of the community from which the Qumran Texts (Dead Sea Scrolls) came. He apparently lived around the middle of the second century B.C.

Salvation: The word means basically health and well-being on all sides of one's life. In salvation one is rescued from all that threatens peace and security. In New Testament usage the word has both a present and a future connotation.

Sanctification: An English word for *holiness* (see above).

Satan: The word means *adversary* or *opposer*. In the Old Testament Satan is an angelic being who acts under the authority of God (Job 1:6-12; 2:1-7; Zechariah 3:1-5). In the intertestamental writings and the New Testament (where he is also called *the devil*), he is a being hostile to God, the originator and embodiment of all evil, who will be slain by God in the end time (Revelation 20:10). His origin is not indicated in the Bible.

Septuagint: The translation of the Old Testament into Greek, begun at the middle of the third century B.C. and completed probably in the second century B.C.

Stoics: Popular Hellenistic and Roman philosophers, who took their name from the porch (*stoa*) where their founder Zeno (340-265 B.C.) taught in Athens. They stressed the acceptance in tranquility of the divine will (fate) and the necessity of practical ethics in life.

Wrath: The wrath of God in the Bible is the requiring side of God's love for the chosen people. God's punishment is meant to be redemptive in both Testaments. Paul saw God's wrath as continuously working in the self-willed, progressive degradation of humankind (Romans 1:18-32) and an ultimate wrath for those who *do not obey the truth, but obey wickedness* (Romans 2:5-9). In Second Thessalonians this wrath is said to consist of separation from the presence of the glorious Lord (1:9).

Yahweh: The name for God introduced by Moses to the Hebrew people (Exodus 6:2-3). It probably means *he causes to be* in the sense that he is the Creator. *Jehovah,* which is not a Hebrew word at all, resulted from a sixth or seventh century A.D. combination by Jewish scholars of YHWH with the vowels of the Hebrew word *Adonai,* meaning *my Lord.* Jews were to say *Adonai* rather than to pronounce the sacred divine name.

Guide to Pronunciation

Aegean: Ah-GEE-an
Antiochus Epiphanes: An-TIGH-oh-cus-Eh-PIH-fah-nees
Aristarchus: Ar-iss-TAR-cus
Barnabas: BAR-nah-bas
Caligula: Cah-LIG-you-lah
Colossae: Cuh-LOSS-eye
Epaphras: Ee-PAF-ras
Epaphroditus: Ee-paf-roh-DIGH-tus
Euodia: You-OH-dee-ah
Gnosticism: NOSS-tih-siz-um
Hellenistic: Heh-leh-NISS-tic
Laodicea: Lay-oh-dih-SEE-ah
Logos: LAW-goss
Macedonia: Maa-seh-DON-nee-ah
Onesimus: Oh-NESS-ih-muss
Pharisee: FAIR-ih-see
Politarch: POL-ih-tark
Praetorium: Pray-TORE-ee-um
Scythian: SIH-thee-an
Silvanus: Sil-VAH-nus
Syntyche: Sin-TIH-kay
Thessalonica: Theh-sah-loh-NIGH-kah
Tychicus: TIH-kih-kus

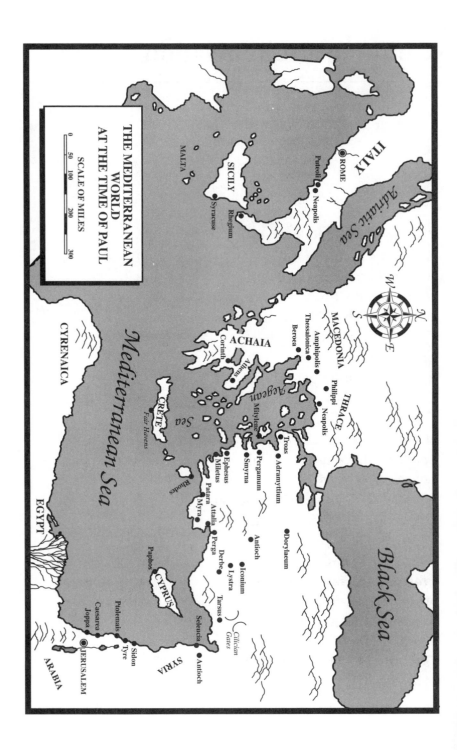

THE MEDITERRANEAN
WORLD
AT THE TIME OF PAUL

SCALE OF MILES

0   50   100   200   300

ITALY

ROME

Puteoli
Neapolis

MALTA

SICILY

Syracuse
Rhegium

Adriatic Sea

MACEDONIA

Beroea
Thessalonica
Amphipolis

ACHAIA
Corinth
Athens

THRACE
Philippi
Neapolis

CRETE
Fair Havens

Aegean
Sea

Mitylene

Troas
Adramyttium

Pergamum
Smyrna
Ephesus
Miletus

Rhodes

Patara
Myra
Attalia
Perga
Derbe

Antioch
Dorylaeum

Iconium
Lystra

Tarsus

Mediterranean Sea

CYRENAICA

EGYPT

Paphos

CYPRUS

Ptolemais
Caesarea
Joppa

Seleucia

Cilician
Gates

SYRIA

Antioch

Sidon
Tyre

JERUSALEM

ARABIA

Black Sea